W9-ADW-696

WATER RESOURCES:
Efficient, Sustainable, and Equitable Use

DATE DUE

APR 2 9 2010	

DEMCO, INC. 38-2931

Water is a prerequisite for life on Earth. Today, approximately a third of the Earth's population suffers because of water scarcity, and by the year 2025, this will most likely rise to two-thirds. This volume shows what conflicts this will entail and provides a basis for possible solutions.

Wolfram Mauser is Professor of Geography and Geographical Remote Sensing at the Ludwig-Maximilian-University of Munich.

Our addresses on the Internet:
www.the-sustainability-project.com
www.forum-fuer-verantwortung.de
[English version available]

TD
345
,M2713
2009

WATER RESOURCES:
Efficient, Sustainable, and Equitable Use

WOLFRAM MAUSER

Translated by Karen Schneider

Klaus Wiegandt, General Editor

HAUS PUBLISHING

KALAMAZOO VALLEY
COMMUNITY COLLEGE
LIBRARY

First published in Great Britain in 2009 by
Haus Publishing Ltd
70 Cadogan Place
London SW1X 9AH
www.hauspublishing.com

Originally published as: FORUM FÜR VERANTWORTUNG, *Wie Lange Reicht die Ressource Wasser?*, by Wolfram Mauser. Ed. by Klaus Wiegandt

© 2007 Fischer Taschenbuch Verlag in der S. Fischer Verlag GmbH, Frankfurt am Main

English translation copyright © Karen Schneider 2008

The moral right of the author has been asserted

A CIP catalogue record for this book
is available from the British Library

ISBN 978-1-906598-07-5

Typeset in Sabon by MacGuru Ltd
Printed in Dubai by Oriental Press

CONDITIONS OF SALE

All rights reserved. No part of this publication may be reproduced, stored in a retrieval system, or transmitted in any form or by any means, electronic, mechanical, photocopying, recording or otherwise, without the prior permission of the publisher.

This book is sold subject to the condition that it shall not, by way of trade or otherwise, be lent, re-sold, hired out or otherwise circulated without the publisher's prior consent in any form of binding or cover other than that in which it is published and without a similar condition including this condition being imposed on the subsequent purchaser.

Mixed Sources
Product group from well-managed
forests and other controlled sources
www.fsc.org Cert no.CU-COC-809367
© 1996 Forest Stewardship Council

Haus Publishing believes in the importance of a sustainable future for our planet. This book is printed on paper produced in accordance with the standards of sustainability set out and monitored by the FSC. The printer holds chain of custody.

Contents

Editor's Foreword

Sales of the German-language edition of this series have exceeded all expectations. The positive media response has been encouraging, too. Both of these positive responses demonstrate that the series addresses the right topics in a language that is easily understood by the general reader. The combination of thematic breadth and scientifically astute, yet generally accessible writing, is particularly important as I believe it to be a vital prerequisite for smoothing the way to a sustainable society by turning knowledge into action. After all, I am not a scientist myself; my background is in business.

A few months ago, shortly after the first volumes had been published, we received suggestions from neighboring countries in Europe recommending that an English-language edition would reach a far larger readership. Books dealing with global challenges, they said, require global action brought about by informed debate amongst as large an audience as possible. When delegates from India, China, and Pakistan voiced similar concerns at an international conference my mind was made up. Dedicated individuals such as Lester R. Brown and Jonathan Porritt deserve credit for bringing the concept of sustainability to the attention of the general public, I am convinced that this series can give the discourse about sustainability something new.

Two years have passed since I wrote the foreword to the initial German edition. During this time, unsustainable developments on our planet have come to our attention in ever more dramatic ways. The price of oil has nearly tripled; the value of industrial metals has risen exponentially and, quite unexpectedly, the costs of staple foods such as corn, rice, and wheat have reached all-time highs. Around the globe, people are increasingly concerned that the pressure caused by these drastic price increases will lead to serious destabilization in China, India, Indonesia, Vietnam, and Malaysia, the world's key developing regions.

The frequency and intensity of natural disasters brought on by global warming has continued to increase. Many regions of our Earth are experiencing prolonged droughts, with subsequent shortages of drinking water and the destruction of entire harvests. In other parts of the world, typhoons and hurricanes are causing massive flooding and inflicting immeasurable suffering.

The turbulence in the world's financial markets, triggered by the US sub-prime mortgage crisis, has only added to these woes. It has affected every country and made clear just how unscrupulous and sometimes irresponsible speculation has become in today's financial world. The expectation of exorbitant short-term rates of return on capital investments led to complex and obscure financial engineering. Coupled with a reckless willingness to take risks everyone involved seemingly lost track of the situation. How else can blue chip companies incur multi-billion dollar losses? If central banks had not come to the rescue with dramatic steps to back up their currencies, the world's economy would have collapsed. It was only in these circumstances that the use of public monies could be justified. It is therefore imperative to prevent a repeat of speculation with short-term capital on such a gigantic scale.

Taken together, these developments have at least significantly improved the readiness for a debate on sustainability. Many more are now aware that our wasteful use of natural resources and energy have serious consequences, and not only for future generations.

Two years ago, who would have dared to hope that WalMart, the world's largest retailer, would initiate a dialog about sustainability with its customers and promise to put the results into practice? Who would have considered it possible that CNN would start a series "Going Green"? Every day, more and more businesses worldwide announce that they are putting the topic of sustainability at the core of their strategic considerations. Let us use this momentum to try and make sure that these positive developments are not a flash in the pan, but a solid part of our necessary discourse within civic society.

However, we cannot achieve sustainable development through a multitude of individual adjustments. We are facing the challenge of critical fundamental questioning of our lifestyle and consumption and patterns of production. We must grapple with the complexity of the entire earth system in a forward-looking and precautionary manner, and not focus solely on topics such as energy and climate change.

The authors of these twelve books examine the consequences of our destructive interference in the Earth ecosystem from different perspectives. They point out that we still have plenty of opportunities to shape a sustainable future. If we want to achieve this, however, it is imperative that we use the information we have as a basis for systematic action, guided by the principles of sustainable development. If the step from knowledge to action is not only to be taken, but also to succeed, we need to offer comprehensive education to all, with the foundation in early childhood. The central issues of the future must be anchored firmly in school curricula, and no university student should be permitted to graduate without having completed a general course on sustainable development. Everyday opportunities for action must be made clear to us all – young and old. Only then can we begin to think critically about our lifestyles and make positive changes in the direction of sustainability. We need to show the business community the way to sustainable development via a responsible attitude to consumption, and become active within our sphere of influence as opinion leaders.

For this reason, my foundation *Forum für Verantwortung*, the ASKO EUROPA-FOUNDATION, and the European Academy Otzenhausen have joined forces to produce educational materials on the future of the Earth to accompany the twelve books developed at the renowned Wuppertal Institute for Climate, Environment and Energy. We are setting up an extensive program of seminars, and the initial results are very promising. The success of our initiative "Encouraging Sustainability," which has now been awarded the status of an official project of the UN Decade "Education for Sustainable Development," confirms the public's great interest in, and demand for, well-founded information.

I would like to thank the authors for their additional effort to update all their information and put the contents of their original volumes in a more global context. My special thanks goes to the translators, who submitted themselves to a strict timetable, and to Annette Maas for coordinating the Sustainability Project. I am grateful for the expert editorial advice of Amy Irvine and the Haus Publishing editorial team for not losing track of the "3600-page-work."

Taking Action – Out of Insight and Responsibility

"We were on our way to becoming gods, supreme beings who could create a second world, using the natural world only as building blocks for our new creation."

This warning by the psychoanalyst and social philosopher Erich Fromm is to be found in *To Have or to Be?* (1976). It aptly expresses the dilemma in which we find ourselves as a result of our scientific-technical orientation.

The original intention of submitting to nature in order to make use of it ("knowledge is power") evolved into subjugating nature in order to exploit it. We have left the earlier successful path with its many advances and are now on the wrong track, a path of danger with incalculable risks. The greatest danger stems from the unshakable faith of the overwhelming majority of politicians and business leaders in unlimited economic growth which, together with limitless technological innovation, is supposed to provide solutions to all the challenges of the present and the future.

For decades now, scientists have been warning of this collision course with nature. As early as 1983, the United Nations founded the World Commission on Environment and Development which published the Brundtland Report in 1987. Under the title *Our Common Future*, it presented a concept that could save mankind from catastrophe and help to find the way back to a responsible way of life, the concept of long-term environmentally sustainable use of resources. "Sustainability," as used in the Brundtland Report, means "development that meets the needs of the present without compromising the ability of future generations to meet their own needs."

Despite many efforts, this guiding principle for ecologically, economically, and socially sustainable action has unfortunately not yet become the reality it can, indeed must, become. I believe the reason for this is that civil societies have not yet been sufficiently informed and mobilized.

Forum für Verantwortung

Against this background, and in the light of ever more warnings and scientific results, I decided to take on a societal responsibility with my foundation. I would like to contribute to the expansion of public discourse about sustainable development which is absolutely essential. It is my desire to provide a large number of people with facts and contextual knowledge on the subject of sustainability, and to show alternative options for future action.

After all, the principle of "sustainable development" alone is insufficient to change current patterns of living and economic practices. It does provide some orientation, but it has to be negotiated in concrete terms within society and then implemented in patterns of behavior. A democratic society seriously seeking to reorient itself towards future viability must rely on critical, creative individuals capable of both discussion and action. For this reason, life-long learning, from childhood to old age, is a necessary precondition for realizing sustainable development. The practical implementation of the ecological, economic, and social goals of a sustainability strategy in economic policy requires people able to reflect, innovate and recognize potentials for structural change and learn to use them in the best interests of society.

It is not enough for individuals to be merely "concerned." On the contrary, it is necessary to understand the scientific background and interconnections in order to have access to them and be able to develop them in discussions that lead in the right direction. Only in this way can the ability to make appropriate judgments emerge, and this is a prerequisite for responsible action.

The essential condition for this is presentation of both the facts and the theories within whose framework possible courses of action are visible in a manner that is both appropriate to the subject matter and comprehensible. Then, people will be able to use them to guide their personal behavior.

In order to move towards this goal, I asked renowned scientists to present in a generally understandable way the state of research and the possible options on twelve important topics in the area of sustainable development in the series "*Forum für Verantwortung.*" All those involved in this project are in agreement that there is no alternative to a united path of all societies towards sustainability:

— *Our Planet: How Much More Can Earth Take?* (Jill Jäger)
— *Energy: The World's Race for Resources in the 21st Century* (Hermann-Joseph Wagner)
— *Our Threatened Oceans* (Stefan Rahmstorf and Katherine Richardson)
— *Water Resources: Efficient, Sustainable and Equitable Use* (Wolfram Mauser)
— *The Earth: Natural Resources and Human Intervention* (Friedrich Schmidt-Bleek)
— *Overcrowded World? Global Population and International Migration* (Rainer Münz and Albert F. Reiterer)
— *Feeding the Planet: Environmental Protection through Sustainable Agriculture* (Klaus Hahlbrock)
— *Costing the Earth? Perspectives of Sustainable Development* (Bernd Meyer)

- *The New Plagues: Pandemics and Poverty in a Globalized World* (Stefan Kaufmann)
- *Climate Change: The Point of No Return* (Mojib Latif)
- *The Demise of Diversity: Loss and Extinction* (Josef H Reichholf)
- *Building a New World Order: Sustainable Policies for the Future* (Harald Müller)

The public debate

What gives me the courage to carry out this project and the optimism that I will reach civil societies in this way, and possibly provide an impetus for change?

For one thing, I have observed that, because of the number and severity of natural disasters in recent years, people have become more sensitive concerning questions of how we treat the Earth. For another, there are scarcely any books on the market that cover in language comprehensible to civil society the broad spectrum of comprehensive sustainable development in an integrated manner.

When I began to structure my ideas and the prerequisites for a public discourse on sustainability in 2004, I could not foresee that by the time the first books of the series were published, the general public would have come to perceive at least climate change and energy as topics of great concern. I believe this occurred especially as a result of the following events:

First, the United States witnessed the devastation of New Orleans in August 2005 by Hurricane Katrina, and the anarchy following in the wake of this disaster.

Second, in 2006, Al Gore began his information campaign on

climate change and wastage of energy, culminating in his film *An Inconvenient Truth*, which has made an impression on a wide audience of all age groups around the world.

Third, the 700-page Stern Report, commissioned by the British government, published in 2007 by the former Chief Economist of the World Bank Nicholas Stern in collaboration with other economists, was a wake-up call for politicians and business leaders alike. This report makes clear how extensive the damage to the global economy will be if we continue with "business as usual" and do not take vigorous steps to halt climate change. At the same time, the report demonstrates that we could finance countermeasures for just one-tenth of the cost of the probable damage, and could limit average global warming to 2° C – if we only took action.

Fourth, the most recent IPCC report, published in early 2007, was met by especially intense media interest, and therefore also received considerable public attention. It laid bare as never before how serious the situation is, and called for drastic action against climate change.

Last, but not least, the exceptional commitment of a number of billionaires such as Bill Gates, Warren Buffett, George Soros, and Richard Branson as well as Bill Clinton's work to "save the world" is impressing people around the globe and deserves mention here.

An important task for the authors of our twelve-volume series was to provide appropriate steps towards sustainable development in their particular subject area. In this context, we must always be aware that successful transition to this type of economic, ecological, and social development on our planet cannot succeed immediately, but will require many decades. Today, there are still no sure formulae for the most successful long-term path. A large number of scientists and even more innovative entrepreneurs and managers will have to use their creativity and dynamism to solve the great challenges. Nonetheless, even today, we can discern the first clear goals we must reach in order to avert a looming catastrophe. And billions of consumers around the world can use their daily purchasing decisions to help both ease and significantly accelerate the economy's transition to sustainable development – provided the political framework is there. In addition, from a global perspective, billions of citizens have the opportunity to mark out the political "guide rails" in a democratic way via their parliaments.

The most important insight currently shared by the scientific, political, and economic communities is that our resource-intensive Western model of prosperity (enjoyed today by one billion people) cannot be extended to another five billion or, by 2050, at least eight billion people. That would go far beyond the biophysical capacity of the planet. This realization is not in dispute. At issue, however, are the consequences we need to draw from it.

If we want to avoid serious conflicts between nations, the industrialized countries must reduce their consumption of resources by more than the developing and threshold countries increase theirs. In the future, all countries must achieve the same level of consumption. Only then will we be able to create the necessary ecological room for maneuver in order to ensure an appropriate level of prosperity for developing and threshold countries.

To avoid a dramatic loss of prosperity in the West during this long-term process of adaptation, the transition from high to low resource use, that is, to an ecological market economy, must be set in motion quickly.

On the other hand, the threshold and developing countries must commit themselves to getting their population growth under control within the foreseeable future. The twenty-year

Programme of Action adopted by the United Nations International Conference on Population and Development in Cairo in 1994 must be implemented with stronger support from the industrialized nations.

If humankind does not succeed in drastically improving resource and energy efficiency and reducing population growth in a sustainable manner – we should remind ourselves of the United Nations forecast that population growth will come to a halt only at the end of this century, with a world population of eleven to twelve billion – then we run the real risk of developing eco-dictatorships. In the words of Ernst Ulrich von Weizsäcker: "States will be sorely tempted to ration limited resources, to micromanage economic activity, and in the interest of the environment to specify from above what citizens may or may not do. 'Quality-of-life' experts might define in an authoritarian way what kind of needs people are permitted to satisfy." (*Earth Politics*, 1989, in English translation: 1994).

It is time

It is time for us to take stock in a fundamental and critical way. We, the public, must decide what kind of future we want. Progress and quality of life is not dependent on year-by-year growth in per capita income alone, nor do we need inexorably growing amounts of goods to satisfy our needs. The short-term goals of our economy, such as maximizing profits and accumulating capital, are major obstacles to sustainable development. We should go back to a more decentralized economy and reduce world trade and the waste of energy associated with it in a targeted fashion. If resources and energy were to cost their "true" prices, the global process of rationalization and labor displacement will be reversed, because cost pressure will be shifted to the areas of materials and energy.

The path to sustainability requires enormous technological innovations. But not everything that is technologically possible has to be put into practice. We should not strive to place all areas of our lives under the dictates of the economic system. Making justice and fairness a reality for everyone is not only a moral and ethical imperative, but is also the most important means of securing world peace in the long term. For this reason, it is essential to place the political relationship between states and peoples on a new basis, a basis with which everyone can identify, not only the most powerful. Without common principles of global governance, sustainability cannot become a reality in any of the fields discussed in this series.

And finally, we must ask whether we humans have the right to reproduce to such an extent that we may reach a population of eleven to twelve billion by the end of this century, laying claim to every square centimeter of our Earth and restricting and destroying the habitats and way of life of all other species to an ever greater degree.

Our future is not predetermined. We ourselves shape it by our actions. We can continue as before, but if we do so, we will put ourselves in the biophysical straitjacket of nature, with possibly disastrous political implications, by the middle of this century. But we also have the opportunity to create a fairer and more viable future for ourselves and for future generations. This requires the commitment of everyone on our planet.

Klaus Wiegandt
Summer 2008

Preface

When Klaus Wiegandt approached me and told me about his plans to publish a twelve-volume series on sustainability through his foundation and asked me if I wanted to be part of it, I did not hesitate in agreeing. In my judgment, the issue of water supplies is too important, in particular in the context of sustainability, to be swallowed up in highly complex scientific discussions and in newspaper articles that are often too superficial to handle such complex issues adequately. Thus, we aimed at a book on the future of water that is understandable to the general reader, but also scientifically sound, a book that would present today's knowledge about the opportunities and risks on the common path to a sustainable use of fresh water.

My initial enthusiasm for this task was quickly followed by respect for the subject of this book, water. It is the kind of respect that arises, comparable to experiencing a helicopter flight, from realizing the range and complexity of an issue, which scientists usually and inevitably only deal with in small and clearly defined sections.

Water is a central resource for nature, life, and people. What we want to know about water and how we handle it, can tell us a lot about ourselves: about our difficulties in using water as a renewable and yet finite resource, about our problems in really imagining a world in which we live as part of nature, and about our immense resourcefulness, yet at the same time, our immense short-sightedness. Thus, dealing with water is also dealing with our often problematic relationship with nature.

Water – this substance that dissolves almost everything – has also, almost without my noticing it, slowly dissolved the boundaries between scientific disciplines in the course of my academic career. Gradually, the question of the purpose of rain joined the question of the cause of rain, on an equal footing. We can only achieve balance between man and nature if the natural sciences, engineering, humanities, social and cultural sciences, as well as economics, work together to address water issues impartially, and thus pave the way to a sustainable use of this natural resource. At times, the arrogance and lack of communication between natural scientists and engineers are not conducive to finding a solution. A solid grounding in the humanities acquired during my upbringing has helped me, as a physicist and geographer, to perceive this.

How to deal with water sustainably (and this is true for all other natural resources) is not a problem that society can simply hand over to the scientists, politicians or economists to solve. This is a crucial question for our emerging globalized culture, which concerns everyone and will determine our survival.

I would like to thank all those who have contributed to the creation of this book. First and foremost, I wish to thank Klaus Wiegandt and the Foundation for Sustainability (*Forum für Verantwortung*) for the vision and courage to approach the subject of sustainability in such a comprehensive manner. This book would not have been possible without the long years of intensive discussions with my colleagues. Here, I am indebted to my colleagues, both former and current, in the National Committee for Global Change Research of the German Research Foundation (DFG) and the BMBF (www.nkgcf.org), which I have chaired for several years now, and I wish to thank them for the manifold, interdisciplinary and always constructive discussions that have produced many new insights. My thanks also go to all my colleagues and staff at the Department for Geography at the LMU Munich for thought-stimulating talks, debates, and support. My greatest appreciation and thanks go to my wife, Dr. Heike Bach, who has lovingly supported me both personally and professionally.

Munich, 20 January 2007

1 Introduction

Water is a natural part of our environment. In our latitudes, i.e. in Northern Europe, water is not scarce and is thus almost taken for granted. In addition to rainwater, which nature provides in abundance, man has set up an intricate water supply system. It ensures that water flows out of the tap with just one twist and can be used for a wide variety of purposes from washing to watering the garden. The apparent success stories about increasingly clean bodies of water and copious fish stocks in our lakes and rivers seem to prove right all those who said that the environmental crises of the last century have been conquered. In brief, at first it looks as if there is no reason to be concerned about water.

In Germany for example, in the Sixties and Seventies, the focus was on the consequences of uninhibited use of water. Since then, the focus has changed radically to global issues in general and specifically on how environmental problems are perceived. The focus then was on polluters and pollution, on dying fish and foul-smelling chemicals, on the cost to the economy of eliminating water pollution, developing and installing appropriate technology such as sewage treatment plants in order to eliminate industrial and domestic pollution. Previously unheard-of ideas were put into practice, for example equipping every town with a sewage treatment plant or the construction of the first enormous industrial sewage treatment plant by BASF in Ludwigshafen. On the whole, success in this area has been considerable, as can be measured by the fact that in the meantime, the topic of water pollution has almost disappeared from public debate on man's relationship with nature. Only floods still cause public concern, from the German perspective above all in connection with the widely-debated consequences of climate change.

In the meantime, our world has not stood still. Industries are now highly internationalized and economic integration is no longer merely European, but global. That humans are responsible for global climate change that affects us all is now undeniable. Computers have advanced beyond the capability of guiding a small three-man capsule to the Moon. Through complex simulations, they provide us with well-grounded foresight based on painstaking and precise hindsight.

Thus, it is worthwhile to lay aside for a while our regional perceptions concerning the Earth's water, which are often based on outdated concepts, and direct our thoughts towards worldwide conclusions about the water situation in today's world. This perspective may be read as:

"The world's fresh water resources are under increasing pressure. Growth in population, increased economic activity and improved standards of living lead to increased competition for and conflicts over limited fresh water resources. A combination of social inequity, economic marginalization and lack of poverty alleviation programs also force people living in extreme poverty to overexploit soil and forestry resources, which often results in negative impacts on water resources . . . It is estimated that currently one-third of the world's population live in countries that experience medium to high water stress. This ratio is expected to grow to two-thirds by 2025."

Thus reads the bleak-sounding summary by the Global Water Partnership (2000), the leading association of international organizations that deal with water. The Global Water

Partnership's conclusions clearly illustrate that perspectives have changed in the last thirty-five years. Firstly, through globalization, the conception of water problems has not only also been globalized, but fundamentally changed. Talk is no longer just of dead fish and bad smells, but also of soils, forests, conflicts, sustainability, and fighting poverty. And it warns that even larger problems may loom on the horizon. The statement by the Global Water Partnership is short and succinct. Although it specifies the problems and their causes, at first it seems to suggest that there are only a few possible solutions.

In the meantime, as a result of extensive modeling with highly developed simulation programs, the global conclusions of the Global Water Partnership are now available on a regional scale. These results indicate where water scarcity is expected to arise in future. The world map shown in Fig. 1 shows probable water scarcity in 2025. The map was created by the International Water Management Institute (IWMI) in Sri Lanka and shows that large parts of the Earth have either economical or physical water scarcity. Economic water scarcity means that in the countries indicated, the shortage of water leads to negative consequences in the economic development of the country, while physical water scarcity means that there is objectively too little water available to supply humans and nature. The affected countries are in the south and in the large developing regions of Asia, whereas in the north, these investigations show there is hardly any water scarcity. The shaded areas indicate regions that will have to import more than 10% of their required grain in the future, mainly due to water scarcity.

Fig. 1 shows that the water problems represented will probably become worldwide problems in the next twenty years. Thus, questions arise, such as were these problems around thirty-five years ago? If so, why were they not dealt with back then? Is this

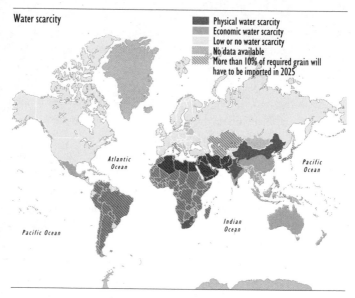

Water scarcity

- Physical water scarcity
- Economic water scarcity
- Low or no water scarcity
- No data available
- More than 10% of required grain will have to be imported in 2025

Atlantic Ocean

Pacific Ocean

Pacific Ocean

Indian Ocean

Figure 1   Map of areas that will most likely suffer from physical and economic water scarcity in 2025 (after Geographie [2007], changed according to IWMI [2000])

account of the problems perhaps only the result of a changed viewpoint, are they perhaps not really so urgent and only an example of the increasing scaremongering in environmental discussions? If these problems have actually only come about in the last thirty to fifty years, new questions then arise. What are the causes of these dramatic water shortages? After all, water is one of the most important natural resources. What are the reasons for the limits of water availability, and where are these limits? How can the future development of water use be designed so that it is fair for all generations, i.e. sustainable?

The radical analyses by the Global Water Partnership and

the IWMI demonstrate that the unrestricted use of the Earth's natural resources by humans will apparently lead, first and foremost, to problems with water resources. The availability of water will reach strict limits in the near future. This gradually increasing consciousness of the limits to water availability is new. Dealing with this new consciousness is a characteristic feature of the debate on environmental issues that came about at the beginning of the 21st century. In addition, because constraints are also appearing in other areas, such as in our energy supply, soil fertility, and marine productivity, it is worth taking a renewed closer look at how humans handle fresh water, their central natural resource. We need to look at our dependence upon its delivery and use, and the conflicts that arise from them.

Before we take an in-depth look at the influence and impact of humans on the water balance of the Earth, as well as the possibilities for future sustainable use of water resources, a discussion of the basics is appropriate. Firstly, the role that water plays on Earth will be discussed, without focusing too much on humans. After all, over billions of years, life formed and developed on Earth without the help of humans, due to the availability of water. What are the consequences due to the extreme, unusual abundance of water, and above all, to its astounding diversity of occurrence on Earth? What would the Earth look like if there were no water? How are water and life linked?

2 Water in the Global Life-Support System of the Earth

Humans live on the Blue Planet. The oceans make our Earth look blue against the black background of space. No other planet that we know of has such a large quantity of water. Traces of frozen water have been found on Mars and there is good reason to believe that rivers and lakes once existed there, but 70% of the Earth's surface is covered with water in its liquid state and another 5% with ice. Water can be found in all three phases on this planet. It is this large amount and multiple states of water that differentiates the Earth from all other known planets.

On Earth, water is always in motion and is part of a cycle that is driven by the energy of the Sun. This leads to the evaporation of water, to condensation, and to precipitation, as well as streamflow and groundwater flow. In comparison to the total water on Earth, only a mere 0.1% participates in the short-term water cycle that is relevant for human consumption. Most water is stored in the oceans, ice caps, and groundwater aquifers and moves only in timescales of several thousands of years or more. The short-term part of the water cycle distributes water on Earth and thus provides water for nature and humans. Fig. 2 shows this short-term water cycle with its numerous transport paths.

It can clearly be seen that water is present in all areas of the natural environment and moves through all components of the Earth system. Water moves as water vapor in the atmosphere, infiltrates the soil as precipitation, flows through the ground as

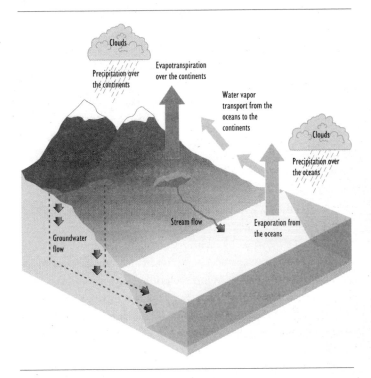

Figure 2　The water cycle of the Earth and its components

Evaporation from the oceans (450,000 km³/a). Precipitation over the oceans
(410,000 km³/a). Water vapor transport from the oceans to the continents
(40,000 km³/a). Evapotranspiration over the continents (70,000 km³/a).
Precipitation over the continents (110,000 km³/a). Streamflow (28,000 km³/a).
Groundwater flow (12,000 km³/a). (After Shiklomanov, 1997).

groundwater, is absorbed by the roots of plants, moves through
the plants, leaves them as water vapor and moves into the atmosphere again, where it is transported by the wind through the
atmosphere until it condenses in clouds and falls as precipitation, thus closing the water cycle.

In its path through the soil, water transports chemical substances, which are either used by plants as nutrients or must be disposed of as waste products. Thus, water is a unique link and intermediary between the different parts of the Earth.

2.1   Water – a unique substance

What are the properties that give water this central intermediary role? What follows shows that water, in comparison to other substances in nature, combines a set of extraordinary properties, which explain the exceptional role that water plays on Earth.

Of those molecules that are most abundant on Earth, water is one of the lightest. In addition, being made up of only three atoms, it has a simple set-up, one oxygen atom and two hydrogen atoms at an angle of 104.5° to each other. This simple molecule has several exceptional properties that are all the result of the fact that one large oxygen atom forms a bond with two very small hydrogen atoms, the smallest atom that exists. Oxygen is the dominant partner and attracts the hydrogen electrons, which leads to the unusually strong polarity of the water molecule, which has definite positive and negative poles. The strength of the polarity of a molecule is expressed in the relative dielectric constant. Of all natural substances, water has the largest dielectric constant. This, together with the small size of the water molecule, is the reason why water is the best known natural solvent. Table 1 illustrates the exceptional position of the relative dielectric constant of water, which is forty times larger than comparable substances in nature.

The exceptional polarity of the water molecule is why water molecules are attracted to each other and form hydrogen bonds, as shown in Fig. 3.

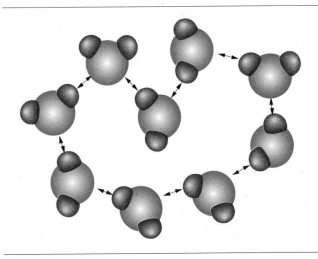

Figure 3   Water molecules bind to each other by forming hydrogen bonds

Substance	Relative dielectric constant
Water	81
Alcohol	5
Soil	2–3
Vacuum	1

Table 1   Relative dielectric constant of water in comparison to other natural substances

This in turn leads to water's exceptionally high melting and boiling points, as compared to oxygen's direct neighbors in the Periodic Table, the elements sulfur, selenium, and tellurium, which can also form similar molecules. Table 2 illustrates the fact that water, as compared to its relatives, should actually have

Molecule	Molecular weight [mol]	Melting point [°C]	Boiling point [°C]
H_2O	18	0	100
H_2S	34	−82	−61
H_2Se	80	−64	−42
H_2Te	129	−51	− 4

Table 2 Comparison of water's melting and boiling points with other similar molecules in nature.

a melting point of -93°C and a boiling point of -72°C. Were this the case, then water could only exist as water vapor on Earth. Instead, due to the mutual electrical attraction between the water molecules, known as hydrogen bonding, water has the well-known melting point of 0°C and boiling point of 100°C. It is obvious that although water is clearly lighter than its relatives, it melts and boils at much higher temperatures. Hydrogen bonds are responsible for an additional physical property of water that is important for the Earth system: water's extremely high heat capacity and high vaporization and fusion temperatures. Large amounts of heat are needed to melt or vaporize water and are thus stored in the water molecule, as in all comparable known natural substances. This excellent capacity for heat storage is important not just in nature, but is also utilized by humans to cool machinery. In order to melt ice, 340 J/g is needed and 2450 J/g is needed to vaporize water. This heat is stored in the water and is set free by condensation or freezing respectively.

However, all these exceptional properties of water take on even more importance when the position of the Earth in our planetary system is considered, as shown in Fig. 4. This shows the phase diagram of water, with several planets of our solar system plotted. If temperature is plotted against pressure, water

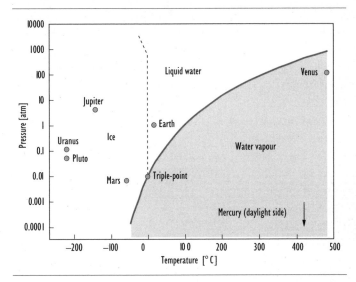

Figure 4   Phase diagram of water with the position of each respective planet

According to this diagram, liquid water can only exist on Earth

is solid, liquid, or gaseous at every point in the graph. As can be seen, water occurs as a liquid only on Earth. This is due to the prevailing atmospheric pressure or to the temperature or to both. The atmosphere of Venus is too hot and too dense for rain, while the other planets are too cold.

Why is liquid water such an important factor in understanding the exceptional role that Earth plays in our solar system?

The complex properties of water presented here, together with the simultaneous occurrence of water in its liquid form, ideally fit the requirements necessary for carbon-based life. Therefore, it is unsurprising that all life forms are predominantly made up of liquid water. The three-dimensional structure of the biological macromolecule, which is, among others, the basis for storing genetic information, can only exist due to hydrogen bonds, a unique property of the water molecule and thus only possible in a liquid state. The ambient water molecules in the aqueous solution provide structure and flexibility to the macromolecules of life.

However, it is not only these properties that mean life on Earth is closely linked to water. Another very exceptional property of water has decisively helped life develop, namely its density anomaly. Water has its greatest density at 3.96°C. In contrast to all other known substances, which contract upon cooling, water expands below this temperature and becomes less dense. Thus, bodies of water freeze from the top down and not from the bottom up, since water with a temperature of 3.96°C sinks. For life in lakes, this is a decisive advantage.

2.2 Why are life and water an inseparable unit?

The water cycle is a prerequisite for all life on Earth. However, it is also part of a larger "machine," the Earth system. This is composed of mutually interacting processes and cycles. The carbon, nitrogen, phosphorous, and sulfur cycles are very closely connected to the water cycle. All of these cycles are involved in all life processes, which are probably the most exceptional properties of this planet.

The operability of the Earth system and its linked cycles formed the basis for the emergence of life and are the prerequisite for its preservation. Thus, the functioning cycles on Earth form this planet's life-support system. This life-support system provides climate control by keeping the temperature within a range that is acceptable for life. It ensures a water supply through precipitation and supplies plants with CO_2, water, and nutrients, animals with oxygen, water, and proteins. Through geological and biological processes that weather rocks, it allows nutrients to be released and bacteria to break down waste products, thus purifying the water. The system continually builds up the ozone layer to protect against too much ultraviolet radiation. And, last but not least, organisms undergo mutation and thus adapt to changing living conditions and thus create the necessary diversity. This ensures that in the inconceivably long timespan of the last 2.7 billion years, there has never been a time without life. Thus, the integrity and efficiency of the Earth's life-support system is the most valuable and precious commodity on the planet and must be preserved by all means. Which mechanisms characterize this life-support system?

2.3 The third equilibrium

The occurrence of liquid water on Earth and with it the creation of the water cycle is not a coincidence. In fact, recent research has shown that it is a manifestation of a dynamic equilibrium, which established itself during the evolution of life on Earth and is caused by the interaction of that life with non-living processes.

Assuming that there were no life on Earth, it can be shown (Gorshkov, 2000) that there could only be two stable energy states, which, however, are at very different temperatures. In Fig. 5, they are identified by the minima one and three in the Lyapunov curve. The Lyapunov curve provides information about the average energy content of a square meter of the Earth's surface in relation to the surface temperature. A minimum in the Lyapunov curve characterizes a state of equilibrium that can only be changed if additional external energy is supplied. A lifeless

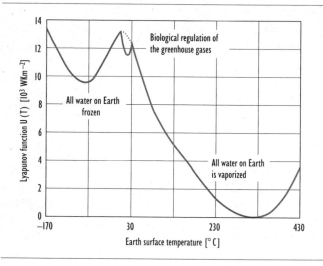

Figure 5 The three equilibrium states of the Earth and their corresponding surface temperatures (after Gorshkov, 2000)

Earth cannot be destabilized through small external changes, i.e. it is in a physically stable state. Examples of these states are an almost completely ice-covered planet with a temperature of -90°C (minimum one in Fig. 5) and one with a temperature of +310°C where all water is vaporized (minimum three in Fig. 5).

In the first case, equilibrium occurs when all greenhouse gases, principally CO_2 and water vapor, are frozen out of the atmosphere and the white ice sheets that cover broad expanses of the surface reflect the Sun's energy almost completely. The absence of greenhouse gases and reflection of solar radiation cause a powerful cooling of the Earth. This state is stable inasmuch as a slight warming (e. g. if the Earth moves closer to the Sun during its orbit) only leads to increased thermal radiation.

This can radiate into space, unhindered by greenhouse gases and the Earth cools accordingly. With no greenhouse gases, only the Sun's energy stops the Earth from cooling down to -273°C —absolute zero.

The second state of physical equilibrium is characterized by having the highest possible effects of the two greenhouse gases. Water vapor is, like CO_2, a powerful greenhouse gas. The highest possible greenhouse effect is achieved if water is only present as water vapor in the atmosphere and thus acts as a greenhouse gas. The CO_2, which is released into the atmosphere through volcanic action, also gradually increases, since there would be no decay processes for atmospheric CO_2 on a lifeless Earth. This leads to a further increase of the greenhouse effect. The extreme greenhouse effect, induced by the high concentrations of water vapor and CO_2 in the atmosphere, leads to a stable state of equilibrium at a surface temperature of around 310°C.

Both of these states of equilibrium in the Earth system are characterized by the fact that neither a water nor a carbon cycle exists. However, neither equilibrium state ever actually occurred on Earth! Why?

Life created a third state at a different temperature level supportive of life, which on a purely physical basis cannot be explained without the influence of the Earth system cycles. Since this state is not possible without life, it follows that life itself created this third stable state with temperatures between 5°C and 25°C, through its additional mechanisms of biological regulation. This third state was gradually achieved in that the incipient photosynthesis at the beginning of life on Earth removed CO_2 from the atmosphere on a large scale, in order to create biomass and limestone. This reduced the greenhouse effect and lowered temperatures. A large part of the CO_2 from the primordial atmosphere was incorporated into the shells and skeletons of those life-forms. When these died, the CO_2 was stored in the rocks of the limestone mountains as calcium carbonate $(CaCO_3)$. The dynamic equilibrium which resulted from this massive restructuring of the atmosphere was characterized by the gradual cooling of the planet to temperatures under 100°C at which water is mainly a liquid and not, as in both states of equilibrium with purely physical causes, a solid or a gas. The CO_2 that is still in the atmosphere is mainly responsible for the greenhouse effect, which warms the Earth by reducing radiation of heat into space.

The third state of equilibrium is connected to life on Earth and would disappear if there were no more life. A further means by which this equilibrium might be stopped is, as seen in Fig. 5, an excessive cooling or heating of the Earth due to an extreme short-term increase or decrease of the atmospheric greenhouse gases. This would mean that the temperature on Earth, which for billions of years has been in the interval within the small valley in Fig. 5, around 15°C, would move out of that interval. The Earth's temperature would thus move inevitably and automatically into the one of the two stable states: -90°C or +310°C.

Thus, the third equilibrium state shown in Fig. 5 is dependent upon a meticulous balance of greenhouse gases on Earth. A key role in this balance is of course the natural regulation of greenhouse gases, especially CO_2 and water vapor. This occurs due to the close interaction of the CO_2 cycle and the water cycle via vegetation. Vegetation is very important in both cycles in many ways:

- Vegetation regulates the CO_2 content of the atmosphere through the assimilation of carbon as well as when plants die by transferring the carbon to long-term reservoirs, such as the deep oceans or the soil.
- Vegetation influences the water vapor content of the

atmosphere through increased evaporation from the vegetation. After rain, when the uppermost soil layer (about 5 cm) is dry again, evaporation from surfaces without vegetation is drastically reduced. However, land plants grow roots in the soil and thus create an efficient transport system which can extract water from the entire root zone in the soil (from 0.3 m to 2 m) and transfer it as water vapor to the atmosphere. The increased water vapor content leads to increased precipitation and thus to more vegetation.

– Vegetation regulates the O_2 content of the atmosphere through the production of oxygen, which in turn is the prerequisite for all decomposers, such as soil bacteria and fungi. These break down dead vegetation, releasing CO_2 and thus returning the carbon that was stored in the plants to the atmosphere, closing the carbon cycle.

Although the carbon and water cycles had only little to do with one another at the beginning of the Earth's development, they are now closely related through vegetation.

The third state of equilibrium is sustained by the planet's life-support system, which, in this context, performs the following functions, among others:

– Through the exchange of CO_2 between the atmosphere and long-term reservoirs such as the oceans and the soil, thus regulating the heat balance through the greenhouse effect and maintaining the Earth's temperature at a level fit for life.

– Through evaporation and with it distillation, ensuring clean water for the rain on the continents. Above all, the oceans are the principal source for evaporating these large amounts of water, which are then transported via the global wind systems to the continents.

- Through weathering, creating soil from rocks and thus providing nutrients for vegetation.
- Through the growth of plants, thus providing food for humans and animals.
- Through the decay of the remains of plants and animals, thus breaking down waste products or turning them into nutrients.

These five functions all require liquid water and thus, their performance is impaired by a lack of water.

The third state of equilibrium has been impressively stable in the course of its three-billion-year history. Its stability is further shown by the fact that in spite of massive external influences, such as meteorite impacts, which were responsible for the extinction of entire species and changes in the Earth's orbit that led to ice ages, the environmental conditions in this time have remained within the limits suitable for life. As a matter of fact, there is no period known when Earth was without life.

Thus, life on Earth has created a new and stable equilibrium, controlled through photosynthesis, which has maintained conditions on Earth suitable for life for about 2.7 billion years. The availability of water in its liquid state is the basic prerequisite for life, as well as for the operation of the Earth's life-support system. It is remarkable that there has never been a point in all this time when the temperature has moved far enough out of the range of the small minimum of the Lyapunov function at just above 0°C (Fig. 5), so that it has moved past the flanks of the parabola and has had to take on one of the other minima, which would mean the destruction of life on Earth. Fig. 5 clearly shows that this state, which the Earth developed during the course of the last 2.7 billion years, is due to the extraordinary interaction of physical and biological factors. Furthermore, this is not simply a matter of course, nor must it have an infinite continued existence. The questions as to which shocks this system can handle without losing its state of equilibrium and thus inevitably falling into one of the states which are hostile to life, are not settled.

2.4 Human life on Earth

Earth's life-support system has also been the life-support system for human life for only the last two million years. People are dependent for their survival upon the continuous availability of goods and services provided by the Earth system, i.e. our natural resources. There is still the general assumption that these natural resources, in contrast to economic, human, or scientific resources, are free and unlimited.

The natural resources available on Earth are a wide range of ostensive resources that are taken for granted (Daily, 1997). They include:

— *Physical processes*, such as the absorption of UV-radiation that protects life, precipitation, infiltration of rainwater into the soil, phosphorus absorption in the soil, erosion, sedimentation, and seed propagation by wind.
— *Chemical processes*, such as the production of oxygen and CO_2 uptake in photosynthesis, photochemical purification of the atmosphere, chemical weathering of rocks, denitrification.
— *Biological processes*, such as photosynthesis and production of proteins, fats, and essential vitamins, pollination of plants, seed propagation by birds, biological pest control, biomass decay, biogenic weathering of rocks, and stabilization of the biosphere through biodiversity.

A little thought experiment, in which it is assumed that in the future, the biosphere's protection against UV radiation that is now provided for free by the ozone layer must be carried out by civilization's technical infrastructure shows the degree in which our society's prosperity is dependent upon nature's products and processes. A depletion of the ozone layer would mean that in order for any vegetation to be able to grow, all of it would have to be protected with an artificial UV-filter, e.g. covered by a plastic film or artificial layer. The effects that such extensive and complicated technical measures would have upon food prices cannot be fully fathomed. The costs would amount to several billion Euros per year, just to feed the population of Europe, on about 60 million hectares of crops. Furthermore, this sum does not include the costs needed to protect the natural vegetation such as forests and wetlands, which are indispensable for producing oxygen and removing CO_2 from the atmosphere.

Similar thought experiments can be carried out to calculate the costs that would occur if the natural pollination of flowers by bees had to be done artificially, or if instead of natural purification of water, sewage plants had to do the whole job. These drastic examples show that every adverse effect on the functionality of the life-support system will lead to a loss in goods and services. At best, these losses could only be made up by expensive technological substitutes. Thus, it is clear that every adverse effect on the functionality of the life support system causes, at least in principle, costs which do not show up in conventional bookkeeping.

Since the dawn of man, humans have used natural resources to improve their living conditions. As long as humans obtained their primary calorie intake only from the resources in their natural environment, they did not differ from other large mammals in their demands upon the life-support system. Due to the fact that large mammals have existed for millions of years without adverse effects upon the Earth system, it can be concluded that their behavior is naturally programmed to be sustainable and the resources upon which they live are not destroyed by their use.

In the beginning, humans used natural resources for hunting and gathering and creating simple tools. Then, with increasing technological development, the use of natural resources extended to include farming, water, and fossil fuels as well as renewable sources of energy, raw materials, and finally also genetic information. It is this capability for technological development and the associated possibilities for making decisions that leads to a targeted changing of the environment that exceeds the impact of other animals. Thus, mankind's impact upon the Earth system is unique. The technological developments that led to the increased use of natural resources was at first guided by the assumption that the Earth's resources were available on so large a scale that there need be no fear that human demands upon them could have negative consequences for the planet as a whole. The increase in population and above all, the change in lifestyle that resulted in a marked increase in the per-capita use of natural resources, put this naive perception of an unlimited capability of the Earth's life-support system strongly into perspective.

The history of the development of human culture is linked with a steady intensification of the use of natural resources.

This is especially obvious in the amount of energy consumed in order to maintain a certain lifestyle. This is shown in Fig. 6 for the development of human societies, from the early hominids, via the hunter-gatherers, to the primitive and advance agricultural societies, up to the industrial and post-industrial societies of today. A person's daily energy consumption has increased more than a hundredfold in the course of 15,000 years of societal development. In addition to the energy that is needed just

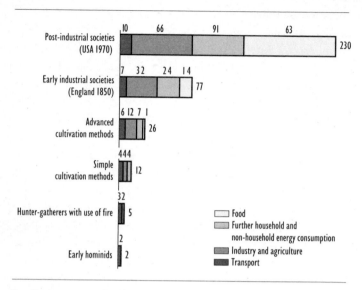

Figure 6   Amount and percentage of energy consumption in 1000 kcal
per person and day for different societies (after Ellen, 1987)

to survive, additional types of energy consumption have come
along through settled living, farming, and transport. Even the
energy consumption that is needed to make food available today
has increased fivefold as compared to our forefathers because of
the high use of energy in modern agriculture.

The increase in energy consumption is easily understood. All
of the cultural products of the last millennia, except those in the
very recent past, were created exclusively by using fossil fuels.
However, when coal, oil, or natural gas are burnt, they are consumed. As they are not renewable, they do not fulfill the criteria
for being part of a cycle.

However, what about the other natural resources whose
use has been also more intensive in the course of our cultural

development? It could be said that water is not used up, since it does not disappear after it is used. Rather, it is continuously renewed in a functioning water cycle. In this sense, as an extreme case, it could be presumed that the water is freely available or, at least with respect to limits on its availability, is fundamentally different from other resources such as fossil fuels. In contrast to the use of non-renewable natural resources, the availability of water is dependent upon the functional efficiency of the water cycle in the Earth system. If this is disturbed, the availability of water is reduced. Water is not the only natural resource that is part of a cycle in the natural Earth system. In addition, oxygen, carbon dioxide, and nutrients, in particular nitrogen, have cycles. Their availability is also dependent upon the functioning of the Earth system, which is made up of a complex interaction of physical and biological processes. Burdens upon these cycles, i.e. extraction, pollution, or diversion of the respective resources, influence the efficiency of the relevant processes and thus have consequences for the efficiency and stability of the Earth's life-support system.

In the course of the increasingly more intensive use of natural resources, as shown in Fig. 6 for energy, the fact that the maintenance of the third, biologically characterized equilibrium and thus the efficiency of the life-support system is not without a price has been effectively ignored. Our "requirements" with respect to natural resources are in direct competition with the "requirements" of Earth's life-support system, which must be fulfilled in order for the dynamic equilibrium in the Earth system to be sustained. As we are using ever-increasing amounts of the relevant natural resources, here water, they are being taken out of the natural life-support system and are being subjected to our own rules and decisions. We must determine whether we are biting the hand that feeds us.

Where are we on the path toward a massive impact upon the planet's life-support system? The changes in climate and resulting consequences such as increased extreme weather events, the degradation of soils as well as the decrease in biodiversity and, last but not least, the increasing scarcity of water resources are signs that the sum of man-made impacts is negatively influencing the efficiency and stability of Earth's life-support system.

What are the performance limits of the life-support system in fulfilling our wants and how far away are we from serious, possibly irreversible, damage to the Earth system? This question is at the core of this book and differs from purely quantitative issues such as whether water will cease to flow out of the tap. In a simple water budget perspective, all water resources may be assumed to be available to satisfy human needs. However, investigations of the efficiency and performance limits of the life-support system require that only those water resources which are not needed to secure the long-term functioning of the life-support system of the Earth be considered for human use and therefore are available for sustainable use by humans.

2.5   What kind of framework does nature provide for using water?

Classical approaches concerning the availability and usage of water resources are based on the water balance equation, which has precipitation on one side as "input." However, this input varies extremely across the world. Fig. 7 shows the worldwide precipitation distribution in millimeters per year (mm/a) and the worldwide population distribution (lower figure).

The large regional imbalance in the precipitation input is noticeable in the upper figure in Fig. 7. It is caused by the global wind system, which transports water vapor in the atmosphere, and by regional factors, such as mountains and heating surfaces, which results in the conversion of the water vapor in the atmosphere into regionally-differing amounts of precipitation. Particularly notable are the equatorial precipitation belt, the regions around the tropics in northern and southern Africa as well as in Australia with little precipitation, areas in the temperate zones with heavy precipitation, and a general tendency for decreasing precipitation with increasing distance from the oceans. Regions with very heavy precipitation can be seen at the western border of the Andes and the northern Rocky Mountains as well as at the southern border of the Himalayas. This regional distribution of mean precipitation occurs because of the given distribution of the continents and the oceans, the given rotation of the Earth as well as the given solar radiation. The fact that different regions on Earth provide strongly different conditions must be respected by nature as well as humans.

The bottom figure in Fig. 7 shows that the availability of precipitation seems to have a direct effect upon the distribution of settlement. High population densities are only realized in areas with enough precipitation. This is clearly seen in China, India, West Africa, and Europe. The general decline in population density from east to west in the USA also corresponds well with the decreasing precipitation. However, there are also large areas on Earth that have high to very high precipitation, where hardly any humans have settled, such as the Congo and the Amazon basin. Thus, the availability of precipitation alone is not sufficient to explain the distribution of population density. Further deliberations are necessary. Let us follow water as it moves through the Earth system and the path that precipitation takes as it falls upon the Earth's surface on its way back to the ocean. It is along this path that water undertakes diverse functions and is used in a variety of different ways.

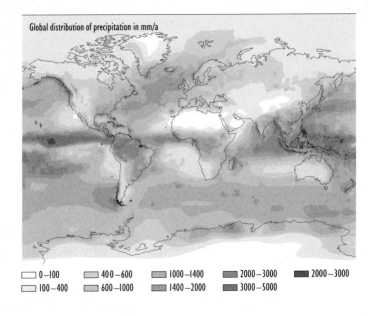

Global distribution of precipitation in mm/a

☐ 0–100		☐ 400–600		☐ 1000–1400		■ 2000–3000		■ 2000–3000	
☐ 100–400		☐ 600–1000		■ 1400–2000		■ 3000–5000			

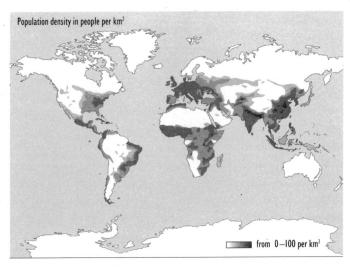

Population density in people per km²

☐ from 0–100 per km³

2.6 Water usage through nature and society

Let us consider the long path that precipitation takes on the Earth's surface. On this path, precipitation is integrated in three important process chains:

- Physical processes. Evaporation and condensation are physical processes. The energy that is needed in the evaporation of water on the Earth's surface is stored in the water vapor in the air and can be transported over great distances and then released through condensation elsewhere. Two-thirds of the planet's entire energy transport occurs via this evaporation and condensation mechanism. It is also responsible for the fact that the temperature is bearable in the center of large land masses.
- Chemical processes. Crystallization, dissolution, and chemical reactions are chemical processes. Water is an extremely good solvent. On geological timescales of millions of years, water wears away mountains, forms soils from bedrock, and sets minerals free, which then flow with the water through the soil and thence to the plants. The minerals serve as natural fertilizers for vegetation and are a prerequisite for its development.
- Biological processes. Photosynthesis is a biological process which transforms CO_2 and water into sugar and oxygen. Both of these are the necessary base products for building all further complex molecules for life on Earth. Ultimately, all secondary products of photosynthesis become the food

Figure 7   Global distribution of the precipitation in mm/a (upper figure) and the population density in people per km2 (lower figure), (UNEP/GRID, 2006).

for bacteria, animals, and humans. By consuming food, water and CO_2 are released again. Thus, water here is also, admittedly in a very indirect way, a transport medium for food in the form of proteins, carbohydrates, and fats.

It is noticeable that, above all, water is used as a mediator substance in the Earth system. To a large degree, the ecosystems on the Earth's surface are responsible for the biological processes of the growth and decay of vegetation and thus for the production of food. They deliver goods to society and provide services. For this, they need, among other things, dissolved substances such as fertilizer, which are provided through chemical processes via water fluxes in the aquatic ecosystems, in the soil, and in groundwater. Aquatic ecosystems also deliver goods such as fish or electricity via water power, but they also provide services such as the decay of dissolved pollutants and thus naturally purify the water. The terrestrial as well as the aquatic ecosystems exchange energy and rainwater through evaporation and condensation.

For humans, society and its well-being are the main points of interest. After all, this book deals with the limits on possible uses of water resources by humans. Society takes water out of the water cycle, in order to use it for a wide range of different purposes. Only a very small part of this water is used up in the sense that it becomes another substance. In fact, typically, on its way through the Earth system, the purity and composition, the aggregate state, or the temperature of the water is changed. Thus, water use is water change. The benefit of use from this change can be manifold. It can be simply drinking the water, to using it in the industrial production of beer, for example, or for industrial cooling processes and thermal electricity plants, for providing electricity by hydroelectric power, transporting water-soluble waste or producing artificial snow for winter tourism.

2.7 Blue and green water

Thus, society benefits from using water directly from bodies of water, lakes, rivers, and groundwater, not only for drinking purposes, but also for washing, industries, transporting waste and for leisure activities. Society also benefits from the indirect use of water, via goods and services that the life-support system of the Earth provides in connection with its own use of water.

The visible, liquid water that flows in rivers, lakes and groundwater is called "blue water" (FAO, 1995, 1997). Therefore, when precipitation falls on the ground, blue water flow can consist of surface flow in channels, on paths, and in streams and rivers. However, it can also be underground flow, in which the groundwater reserves are refilled.

In contrast, the invisible flow of water vapor from the surface into the atmosphere through evaporation from plants is called "green water." This evaporation is called productive green water, since this water flow leads to the production of biomass. Here there is a direct interaction of the water cycle with the carbon cycle here. The productive green water flow is also called transpiration.

Fig. 8 illustrates the path water takes through vegetation using a tree as an example. There are three different areas involved here: the leaves, the trunk, and the roots. Water evaporates predominantly in the leaves, in that energy as sunlight is added to the system and a concentration gradient between the water vapor inside the leaf and in the atmosphere develops. Through small openings in the leaf, called stomata, water vapor can follow the concentration gradient and enter the atmosphere and thus evaporate. However, due to capillary attraction, more water is then pulled from the branches. Therefore, there is a continual water flow through the trunk, which is fed by the root

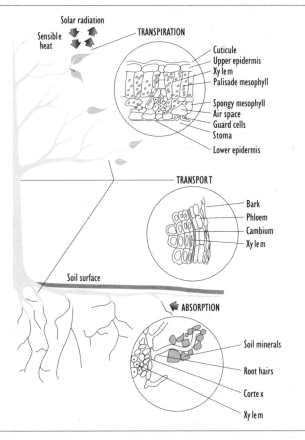

Figure 8   Water's path through vegetation using a tree as an example

hairs in the soil, which in turn absorb the water from the soil.

Plants use water strategically, in order to absorb nutrients from the soil, to cool themselves, and above all to grow through photosynthesis. The stomata in the leaves provide optimal physiological control of the productive green water flow and thus of the plant's water consumption. The stomata open in accordance with the amount of light, temperature, and soil moisture just wide enough to ensure survival and achieve optimal production for the respective location of the plant.

Plants have a root system that, depending on the availability of water and the need for it, develops either shallowly or deeply. They also have a leaf system that is used for evaporation and collecting the necessary energy for photosynthesis. Together, the roots and leaves form an effective bridge that connects the water in the deeper soil layers with the atmosphere.

Since, in order to survive, plants strategically control the productive flow of green water, it is radically different from the purely physical, uncontrolled evaporation from inanimate objects in nature, i.e. from puddles after rain, the ground, wet leaf surfaces, wet roofs, lakes, and rivers. This green water flow is therefore called "unproductive." It is characterized by the fact that, essentially, it only occurs on wet surfaces or in the upper-most layer of the soil. It does not have a root or transport system that collects the water out of a large volume of earth and trans-ports it to the leaves, which are constantly in the Sun. Rather, it is dependent upon the heating of the uppermost layer of the soil and can only evaporate the water from this layer. The vegeta-tion, having developed its root and leaf system in the course of evolution, has a decisive advantage in comparison to inanimate surfaces. This advantage is being able to tap the water supply in the deep soil layers. The root, transport, and evaporation systems are so optimized that the productive green water flow is three times the amount from the same surface area without vegetation (Gorshkov, 2000). This fact plays an important role in the Earth system. Assuming the same amount of precipitation, due to the vegetation, the evaporation of the land surface has increased threefold and the flow in rivers and the groundwater thus correspondingly reduced. Thus, vegetation has decisively changed the water cycle on Earth.

The green water flow includes the water consumption of forests, meadows and rain-fed agriculture, i.e. agriculture that gets its water directly from precipitation. In contrast, the blue water flow characterizes the flow in the aquatic ecosystems of the streams, rivers, lakes, and groundwater, which directly provide humans with water for use. After use, this blue water returns to the aquatic ecosystems as waste water, since it is generally soiled after being used. Blue water is also used for irrigation. Part of the blue water flow then becomes green water flow, when it evaporates from the vegetation. The rest, which does not evaporate, flows back, generally loaded with fertilizers and washed-out soil particles, which causes eutrophication in the lakes and rivers.

The blue and green water flows fulfill important functions in Earth's life support system and provide goods and services that we need to survive and that are important for the development of our societies. They are decisively involved in food production and in the removal and decay of waste products. In this respect, they are not very different in their importance. Thus, why is it nonetheless meaningful to differentiate between blue and green water in our further considerations of water's path through the cycle?

There is a decisive difference between blue and green water, particularly with respect to the use of water resources. This becomes clear if Fig. 9 is examined. The difference is closely causally connected with how blue water moves across the land, i.e. the orientation of the water flow according to the surface gradient. This means that the slope of the surface and the resulting catchment area determines the direction of flow. The blue water, which flows across a surface, follows the slope and converges at one point, the outlet of the catchment area. The slope of the land surface gives the flow of the blue water a characteristic

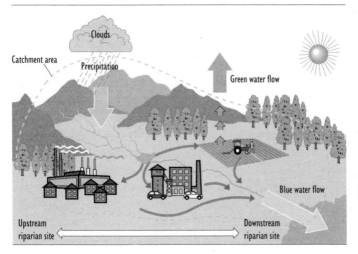

Figure 9   The paths that water takes on the surface

There are two different flow paths that the water from precipitation can take on the surface: the "green" water flow as evaporation and transpiration due to vegetation and the "blue" water flow in rivers and groundwater (after Falkenmark, 2001).

structure and ensures that it can only flow in one direction from every point. Therefore, every location on the surface has a new characteristic, which it would not have without blue water: it is either a downstream or upstream riparian site. The upstream riparian site supplies the water; the downstream riparian site receives and passes the water on. Having upstream and downstream water enables the blue water to be used several times in a given catchment area. For example, water that supports trout in the headwaters of a stream can be used to cool a power station further downstream. In general, however, the reverse is not possible. Water that has been used to cool a power station in the headwaters of a river has only limited utility for raising trout, because then it is too warm. In this case, the upstream usage has hindered further use of the water downstream.

This example demonstrates two characteristics of using blue water: 1) the fundamental potential for multiple usage of blue water due to the given flow paths, and 2) the complex issues that can arise through multiple usage, due to the different requirements of the different uses.

A multiple use of green water in the same catchment area is generally not possible, since green water flow differs fundamentally from blue water flow. This is because after water vapor evaporates into the atmosphere, the water vapor can be transported by the wind out of the catchment area and usually falls as precipitation somewhere far away. Thus, on the surface, green water has upstream riparian sites, but no downstream riparian sites and is lost for further use.

At a later point in this book, we will return to the characteristics of blue water and the differences between it and green water. The concept of blue and green water will prove to be advantageous in a closer analysis of the man-made changes in the water balance and the limits to water usage that exist. The issues dealt with are closely connected with changes in land use and the redirection of the blue water flow to the green water flow connected to them. Through examples, I will demonstrate that a land-use decision is also always a water decision. This will become especially obvious in the next chapter when we look at the Aral Sea and the catchment area of the Nile as regional examples of man-made impact upon the natural water balance. In general, decisions made by an upstream riparian actor also affect a downstream riparian actor. This can be another user, who is capable of voicing his concerns. However, it can also be a natural ecosystem that is involved with purifying the groundwater and which, with its high level of biodiversity, harbors the genetic resources desperately needed for stable further development of the catchment area. Who is actually the concerned party in such cases?

Upstream and downstream riparian actors have different interests and these form the main reason for conflicts over water use between the people involved, as well as those between man-made and natural requirements.

2.8 Summary

Life on Earth has taken possession of two cycles during the course of its development: the carbon cycle and the water cycle. These two cycles, which have little in relation to each other on a lifeless planet, become very closely connected by life. Through billions of years, this close connection has kept the environmental conditions within life-friendly ranges, in that it regulates the concentrations of the most potent greenhouse gases, CO_2 and water vapor. From this, a new and stable temperature equilibrium developed and thus, through increasing biological diversity, the possibility to further stabilize life on Earth. Life itself built its own support system. The further existence of life on Earth, and thus our own existence, is dependent upon the continuous maintenance of life-friendly environmental conditions within the range of the equilibrium that life created. Therefore, disturbing the functional efficiency of the global life-support system through overstraining it must be avoided.

The water cycle on Earth has characteristic properties that can be derived from water as a substance and from its role in supporting life:

1 Precipitation is divided into blue and green water flow. This

division changes if the vegetation or soil is changed.

2   Water is not a non-renewable resource, but rather participates in a cycle. Strictly speaking this is not quite correct, since fossil groundwater also exists. Like natural gas or oil deposits, fossil groundwater has existed for millions of years in hard-to-reach geological layers and is not continually renewed in the water cycle. Although, it is now exploited, it should not play a role in the context of the discussion of the sustainability of water as a natural resource, since it is not renewable and thus in principle its use is not sustainable.

3   Thus, the water that is being considered in this book is continually in motion and flows through all parts of the Earth system, from the atmosphere, on the surface of the land, through the soil, in the groundwater, and in rivers and lakes. The gradient causes clearly defined upstream and downstream riparian relationships.

4   Water assimilates everything that is water-soluble and takes it with it on its way through the Earth system.

The history of mankind is very closely linked to control over the blue water flows in rivers, lakes, and wells. Beginning with the ancient civilizations in China, India, and Mesopotamia, blue water flow has been used for generations for irrigation, for industrialization, for the transportation of waste and for the production of energy. On the other hand, the flow of green water through vegetation is decisively responsible for plant production and for a large amount of goods and services, which Earth's life-support system makes available. Through these primary functions of the water flow in the man-made environment as well as in the biosphere, the water cycle connects human society and nature.

3 How is Water Used? – Regional Examples

In the following chapter, I have selected two examples of water use, which show what water resources are already being subjected to regionally and which problems lead to water scarcity in the regions considered. I will discuss the Aral Sea and the River Nile. Both regions have had massive man-made interventions in their natural water cycles. At the relevant times, these interventions were not carried out carelessly, but after years of planning and numerous investigations. Many of the consequences that skeptics predicted before the projects were undertaken, have occurred. The aim of my discussion is to use the examples to demonstrate the path which has led to the incipient rethinking of these issues.

3.1 The Aral Sea

The example of the Aral Sea demonstrates the problems in centrally planned, large-scale hydraulic engineering projects. Such projects have an ambivalent character: on the one hand, they provide needed additional resources (water for food security, renewable energy) or they protect existing structures and people (flood protection); on the other hand, they can negatively impact the environment and society. The effects of these large-scale projects are rarely only local or regional, but rather can assume even international extents.

The Aral Sea is a so-called terminal lake, a lake without an outlet, i.e. it has no outflow to the ocean. Ecologically, these lakes are very sensitive, since all of the inflow collects and concentrates in the lake, that is, the inflowing water evaporates and leaves the transported pollutant load behind. In principle, this is the same process as in the oceans, where the salt content has built up over billions of years through distillation. In contrast to the oceans, however, the lakes are very small and thus their carrying capacity is much less. The Aral Sea is one of the world's largest terminal lakes. It receives its water from the Pamir and Tian Shan Mountains in the south. Fig. 10 shows its catchment area.

In 1918, the former Soviet Union decided to redirect both rivers that flowed into the Aral Sea, the Amu Darya in the south and the Syr Darya in the northeast, in order to irrigate the desert. The aim of this project was to cultivate rice, grain, melons, and above all cotton. The project was part of a five-year plan and the reason for the project was to cultivate large amounts of cotton – "white gold" – and become a major supplier of cotton on the international market, and they were successful. Since the fall of the Soviet Union, Uzbekistan has become one of the largest cotton producers in the world.

The building of the large-scale irrigation canals for the cotton fields began in the 1930s. Many of the irrigation canals were badly built and thus there was major water loss due to leakage and, due to their open construction, even greater loss due to evaporation. The Qaraqum Canal, the largest in Central Asia, loses between 30 and 70% of its water inflow before it can be used. Today, only an estimated 12% of the irrigation canals in Uzbekistan are leak-proof (UNEP, 2005).

Figure 10 The Aral Sea and its catchment area (from UNEP, 2005)

A sea disappears

When construction was completed in 1960, the unimaginably large amount of 20 to 50 km³ of water, which in earlier times had entered the Aral Sea, was redirected to the fields, where it evaporated as green water. After having lost the major portion of its inflow, in the 1960s the Aral Sea began to shrink.

Fig. 11 shows the start of the redirection of the inflow around 1960 and the resulting reduction of the inflow, which had a direct

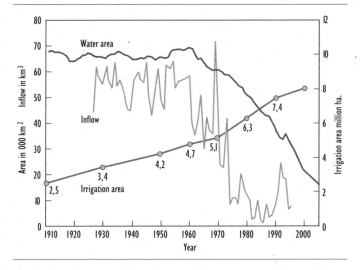

Figure 11 Development of the inflow and the water area of the Aral Sea
as well as the irrigation area from 1910 to today (from
Geographie, 2007)

effect upon the water volume of the Aral Sea. The further course
of development with the steadily increasing irrigation area was
thus set. From 1961 to 1970, the water level of the Aral Sea fell
20 cm per year, the decline increased to 50 to 60 cm per year in
the 1970s and is now at 80 to 90 cm per year. This indicates that
the water used for irrigation has increased unremittingly. The
amount of water taken away from the inflow doubled between
1960 and 1980, which however also led to a doubling in cotton
production. Once again, the close relationship between water
consumption and agricultural production is seen.

The reduction of the inflow led to a rapid shrinking of the
area of the lake, which is impressively shown in the time series
in Fig. 12.

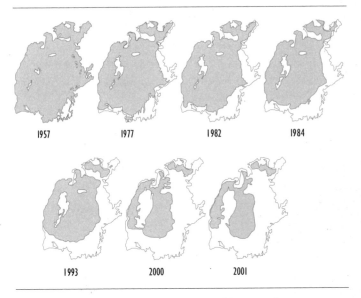

Figure 12 Changes in the area of the Aral Sea (blue area) from 1957 to 2001 (after UNEP, 2002)

The disappearance of the lake was not a surprise to the Soviets; they had actually expected it earlier. At least some of the former Soviet environmental planners were of the opinion that the Aral Sea, as a terminal lake, was one of "nature's mistakes." As early as 1968, a Soviet hydraulic engineer said, "it is obvious that the evaporation of the Aral Sea is unavoidable."

In the meantime, the area of the lake has decreased by approximately 60% and the water volume in the lake by 80%. Although the Aral Sea was the fourth largest lake in the world in the 1960s, it is now the eighth largest and has an area of only 17,000 km².

The reduction of the inflow of the lake was not without consequences for the riparian population. On the one hand, the distance to the water's edge increased as the lake area became smaller. The distillation of the Aral Sea water also led to an increase in the salts, fertilizers, and pesticides in the water. These substances are washed out of the irrigated fields along the upper and middle course of the rivers. In the past 40 years, the salinity of the lake has risen from 10g/1 to 45g/1.

In 1987, the incessant shrinking of the lake led to its separation into two parts: a smaller northern and a southern Aral Sea. In order to mitigate the worst consequences of this partitioning, which prevented a direct exchange of water between the northern and southern lakes, the Soviets built a canal to connect the two lakes. However, this artificial connection was short-lived. Further decreases in the water level in both lakes destroyed the canal in 1999. By 2003, the water level had sunk so low that the southern part of the former Aral Sea divided into two separate lakes itself, a development that was already perceivable in 2001 (see Fig. 12).

Even though groundwater flow from the Pamir and Tianshan Mountains was recently discovered, which supplies the lake with water from the distant mountains and from the leaky irrigation systems, a precise investigation of the amount of transported water has shown that this inflow does not compensate for the losses due to evaporation of the lake.

As with all large-scale operations, further technical measures were tried to equalize and mitigate the negative impacts. Incredibly large amounts of developmental funding were spent plugging the leaks in the irrigation canals on the Syr Darya to save water. In addition, in 2003 the Kazakh parliament decided to build a dam in order to separate the northern and southern parts of the Aral Sea. This was to stop water from the recovering northern Aral Sea, in Kazakhstan, from flowing into the southern Aral Sea and thus seep away into Uzbek territory. There, the seepage water, which is needed in Kazakhstan for the restoration of the lake, would contribute little, due to its small amount in comparison to the larger lake. The dam was put into operation in August 2005. Since then, the water level of the northern lake has risen from 30 meters to 38 meters. Experts there give the lake a future if the water level reaches 42 meters. The lake, which at its smallest, was almost 100 km away from the former harbor city of Aralsk, is now only 25 km away from it.

The fate of the southern Aral Sea is much worse, since it is in the territory of much poorer Uzbekistan. Up to now, the lake has been more or less abandoned and the extent of the destruction is much more serious than in the northern Aral Sea. The shrinkage and drying-up has created extensive salt pans and vegetation has no chance to propagate. It is easy for the fall and winter storms to blow away the salts and pesticides. Up to now, any large-scale attempts to grow vegetation, which would create water vapor through evaporation and thus positively influence the local precipitation as well as reduce the eolian deflation, have failed.

Altogether, the southern Aral Sea is disappearing faster than predicted. At its deepest point, the water has become so heavy due to the high salt content that it no longer mixes with the rest of the lake water nor with the small amount of fresh water inflow. This has fatal consequences, which were not thought of at first. The fresh water floats on top of the salt water and the Sun heats it faster than it would if mixing took place. This increases evaporation and accelerates the disappearance of the lake. The latest investigations based on these results predict that the southern Aral Sea will be completely gone in ten years.

Trading health for cotton

During the course of the shrinking of the Aral Sea, the formerly intact lake ecosystem and its inflow were almost completely destroyed, primarily due to strong salinization. The retreating water left large, salty, and due to the high concentrations of poisonous chemicals, for the most part dead areas. In the meantime, the salts and with them the chemicals have been dispersed by the wind and spread far and wide. Thus, the area around the Aral Sea has been strongly contaminated. The people who live near the lake have serious health problems.

The most important factor that causes the population's health problems is the intense saltiness of the drinking water. Just the salt would not be so bad, but large amounts of chemical fertilizers, pesticides, and defoliants, which were used to improve the cotton crops, have also entered the groundwater in high concentrations. The people have high concentrations of very many agrochemical substances in their bodies: the whole spectrum such as DDT, methyl mercaptophos, ostametyl, dutifos, milbex, hexachlorane, lenacil, and ronit (Ro-Neet). They absorb these poisonous substances through their drinking water and the food chain. Heavy metals and insecticides accumulate especially in fish. Taken in as part of the food chain, high levels of lead, cadmium, and magnesium have been found particularly in children, which have led to birth defects and other disorders. The number of cancer patients has risen alarmingly. In Kyzylorda Oblast, a mid-sized city in the Kazakh part of the lakeside, it has been proven that 800 people contract cancer every year. Above all, they suffer from cancers of the oesophagus and stomach. Investigations have demonstrated a significant correlation between the salt concentration of the drinking water and contracting cancer of the oesophagus.

The miserable quality of the drinking water is the major cause of the high infant mortality in the region, as shown in Fig. 13. In Germany, infant mortality is under twenty children per 1000 live births. The close connection between infant mortality and the

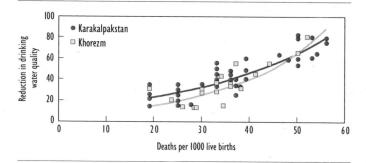

Figure 13 Increase in infant mortality rate as a consequence of contaminated drinking water in two cities in the Aral Sea region

The number of deaths per 1000 live births is plotted horizontally, the decrease in drinking water quality as compared to the legal standards is plotted vertically (100 is the highest measured deviation, UNEP, 2005).

deviation of drinking water quality from the standard in Kazakhstan for the two cities investigated is obvious.

In the major parts of the Aral Sea catchment area, the sanitary conditions and thus the infant mortality rates are comparable with the cities investigated. The main reason for these shocking figures is the inadequate treatment of the drinking water. In the Aral Sea region, in addition to the severe environmental impacts, which were explained above, there is another factor, which is characteristic for other regions with similar problems: the almost complete collapse of the ability of public administrative bodies to fulfil the basic needs of the population. According to the official figures (UNEP, 2005), 8% of the drinking water is not treated at all and more than 60% of the drinking water is not disinfected. More than a sixth of the population is not even connected to the public water supply network and even worse, the state of the water pipes is so bad that large parts of the population have no other choice but to – perhaps not always – but often, get their drinking water from surface water reservoirs or from irrigation systems (Vashneva & Peredkov, 2001). The dire consequences are inevitable: severe diseases of the digestive system.

It is definitely not exaggerating to say that this Aral Sea tragedy, although by necessity only rudimentarily described here, represents the worst man-made water catastrophe in the last forty years. And it is not just a water catastrophe, but rather a catastrophe for mankind. We can assume that the intent of the initiators of the project in the 1920s was not purposely bad or malicious. Yet retrospectively, their idea of changing massive amounts of blue water into green water and thus taking the water away from the Aral Sea, created an inevitable chain of events. In the meantime, the production of large amounts of cotton is pitted against a destroyed ecosystem. However, the most alarming thought is this: the destruction of the ecosystems leads to the impoverishment and destruction of mankind. A spiraling process starts here whose unavoidable end is basically an uninhabitable region: the people involved are forced to exploit the environment that supports them, regardless of the consequences. To survive, they have to buy and use the least expensive fertilizers and pesticides and, increasingly, all principles of sustainability are being ignored. This malpractice degrades the environment, which leads to even more wrongdoing. A downward spiral starts that has no easy way out.

People rarely do things like this out of malice. It is not usually ignorance that starts such downward spirals; generally it is destitution.

3.2 The River Nile

The Nile is one of the largest rivers on Earth. Its catchment area is 3,254,555 km^2. That is approximately 10% of the area in Africa and ten times that of Germany. This area is made up of 1% cities and villages, 2% forests, 3% wetlands, 3% open water bodies, 4% scrub, 5% irrigation areas, 10% agricultural areas without irrigation, 30% desert and 42% savanna grasslands.

More than 250 million people live here today. The annual growth rate is around 2–3% and so the Nile region, together with Bangladesh, belongs to the regions with the highest population growth in the world. Even if the first signs of reduced growth are taken into account, if the growth rate is extrapolated according to demographic rules, the population will pass the 400 million limit in 2025, by about 2030 the population will equal that of the extended EU and by 2060 the population will be around a billion.

The satellite image (overleaf) shows almost all of the Nile catchment area. It stretches from Lake Victoria in the south to the confluence of the White and Blue Nile rivers, exactly in the middle of the image before the large left curve of the river, to the Aswan Dam, to the Nile Valley and the Mediterranean mouth of the river, the Nile delta in the north. The image can tell us quite a lot about the *status quo* for the use of the water resources in this catchment area. Essentially, we can see two areas in the image: the darker part in the south and the lighter part in the north. The dark Nile runs like a band through the light part of the north. This separation of southern Sudan into light and dark areas is not a coincidence. In fact, we are seeing the vegetation at work in the south. The vegetation needs light for photosynthesis and for the evaporation of water. During photosynthesis, the vegetation evaporates water and absorbs sunlight, i.e. it reduces the amount of light that is reflected to the satellite camera, and thus the

image is accordingly darker. The northern part of the image covers the Sahara Desert. Although the information that comes from the different rocks creates different patterns and shades, not even the dark rock areas between the Nile Valley and the Red Sea can absorb so much light as the vegetation in the south, in the black Nile Valley or the water in the Aswan Dam, which can be easily recognized in the image.

Ten countries share the water of the Nile. Of these countries, Eritrea, Tanzania, Uganda, Burundi, Rwanda, Congo, and Kenya are in the south and have a surplus of water. Egypt, Sudan, and parts of Ethiopia are in the north. They have acute water shortages and live off the water that they receive from the southern countries. Therefore, the Nile connects the water-rich areas of the south with their lush tropical vegetation with the water-poor areas of the north, which receive almost no water from precipitation.

The Nile starts at the confluence of the White Nile and the Blue Nile in Sudan. The White Nile rises in the equatorial highlands of Africa, the Blue Nile in the Ethiopian Highlands. Both river branches flow from the African rift at an altitude of 2400 m to their respective lowlands, where the gradient is greatly reduced and large plains are formed.

The source of the Nile is generally taken to be Lake Victoria in Uganda. However, that is only correct if the rivers flowing into Lake Victoria are disregarded. If they are included, the catchment area includes several other countries, including Rwanda and Tanzania. The Nile leaves Lake Victoria through the Ripon Falls in Uganda. After 500 km, the Nile crosses Lake Kyoga (in the image, the braided, black area north of Lake Victoria) and then Lake Albert (the black area to the west of Lake Kyoga). After the Nile leaves Lake Albert, it is called the Albert Nile. Following the terrain, the Nile flows down to the Nile swamps in Sudan (the dark, fan-shaped delta north of Lake Albert). After it leaves the Nile swamps and is joined by a tributary, the Sobat, it becomes the White Nile, so-called because of the large amounts of whitish clay suspended in the water, picked up by the relatively steep gradient in the Sobat. The White Nile flows rather sedately as a mid-sized river from here to Khartoum, where it is joined by the Blue Nile in the middle of the image.

The Blue Nile, sometimes also called the Black Nile, springs from Lake Tana in the Ethiopian Highlands. On its way to Khartoum, it covers 1400 km. One would think that the Blue Nile would be the senior partner in the unification, since it transports 90% of the water and 96% of the Nile's sediment to Khartoum. At any rate, both partners are very different in their behavior, although topographically and climatically, they both spring from quite similar regions.

What is the fundamental difference between the two arms of the Nile?

Both spring from regions that are characterized by both rainy and dry seasons. The rainy season is when the Sun is directly overhead, at its zenith. Then the Sun heats the ground and the heated air rises. Moist air from the surrounding areas flows into the region, bringing severe storms and heavy precipitation. When the Sun moves south, it is dry in the region and the rivers are only fed by the stored water. This is where the fundamental difference between the White and the Blue Nile starts. The Albert Nile flows through a chain of lakes, before it leaves the highlands. It leaves Lake Albert as a constant, uniform river, not bothered by the regular ups and downs in precipitation in the rainy and dry seasons. The White Nile discharge here is between 600 and 1200 m^3/s. Then it flows through the vast Nile swamps in southern Sudan. Here, it loses half of its water due to evaporation and transpiration. Furthermore, the Nile swamps also contribute to the regularity of the discharge of the White Nile, so that after it leaves the swamps, the discharge varies only a little throughout the year.

The story of the Blue Nile on its way to Khartoum is told much more quickly. It has no lakes and swamps on its 1400-km journey. This is the reason for both its fundamental differences from the White Nile: firstly, the water cannot be stored in the Blue Nile and thus, the course of the discharge directly follows that of the precipitation and thus has a rainy and dry cycle. Secondly, in the Blue Nile, the water losses due to the changes from blue into green water resulting from evaporation are low or nonexistent. This explains why the Blue Nile delivers more water than the White Nile and also explains the Nile floods due to the summer rainy season in the tropics. In the rainy season, the Blue Nile is responsible for 70–90% of the total discharge of the Nile and during the dry season, this is reduced to less than 20%.

Figure 14 **The catchment area of the Nile and its hydraulic constructions**
The River Nile is made up of the White Nile, which springs from the African Highlands in Uganda in the south and flows through the lakes in the Sudd, the swamps in lowlands of south Sudan and the Blue Nile, which springs forth from the Ethiopian Highlands in the east and near Khartoum flows together with the White Nile to form the River Nile (Nicol, 2000).

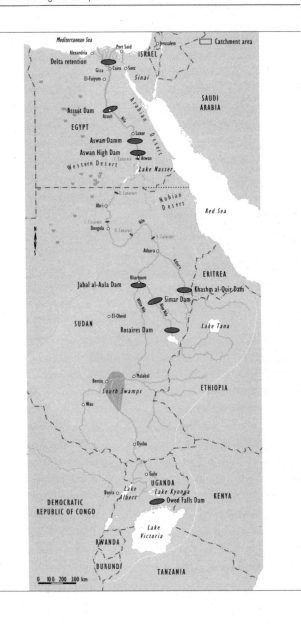

Another little thought experiment, in which we disregard the lakes above the Albert Nile and the swamps in southern Sudan, visualizes the extreme importance this storage has for downstream riparian life. Without this storage, the White Nile would behave similarly to the Blue Nile. This would mean that during the dry season, the Nile would not have its normal discharge. In the dry season of this thought experiment, the Nile would shrink considerably. Even in antiquity, such a small amount of water could not have supported the population of the Nile delta. One can justifiably speculate that without the existence of the reservoir storage, the development of the ancient Egyptian civilization would most likely have been different.

The water of the Nile – consistency in change

Due to the lack of lakes and swamps, the Blue Nile is the reason for the large natural variation in the discharge of the Nile. During the dry season, the Blue Nile carries only a little water. Its discharge rarely exceeds 100 m³/s, even though storage reservoirs have been built in the valleys of the Ethiopian highlands, which can collect the water and release it when needed during the dry season. During the rainy season in August, the discharge of the Blue Nile is frequently over 8000 m³/s. Thus, the annual discharge varies by a factor of eighty, inconceivably high for European rivers. The sediment load of the Blue Nile varies even more between the rainy and dry season. Whereas during the rainy season, large amounts of eroded material are transported out of the Ethiopian highlands, during the dry season levels drop to zero. Learning to cope with this extreme variability was one of the greatest challenges for the population living on the river. If a factory had to cope with such an annual variability in the delivery of its primary products, the first thing it would do would be to build large storage facilities for raw materials needed for production. Only then can the rest of the production factors, such as workforce or energy be utilized throughout the entire year. In this respect, constructing the eight dams shown in Fig. 14 follows the logic of optimal management of the water resources of the Nile.

As difficult as living with the floods was, the annual rhythm of the Nile was of utmost importance for life in ancient Egypt. The stability that the Nile gave the ancient Egyptian civilization that lasted millennia was remarkable. It was a direct consequence of the fertility of the Nile silt, which came with the floods as a result of the rainy season in the tropics, i.e. a completely different part of the Earth provided the fields of the Nile valley with free minerals and fertilizer. Furthermore, the Nile was an ideal trade route for flax and grain. The trading partners and the developing trade system ensured diplomatic relations, which connected Egypt with other countries and cemented its economic power. Furthermore, the farmers then were able to grow more food than they needed, most of all because of the availability of water and the annual renewal of the soil. This surplus could thus be used for society and the military. Therefore, ancient Egypt had little to worry about, especially not that their most valuable resources, the water and the sediments, could be taken away.

Due to its importance for the country, the Nile has also always played a central role in political, social, and religious life. The divine Pharaohs were responsible for the Nile floods, which brought food and life. In reciprocation, the farmers were required to till the soil, to keep the soils fertile, and to tithe a part of their harvest to the Pharaohs. The Pharaohs pledged to use this for social purposes and for the health and well-being of the Egyptian people.

There are no records from the time of the Pharaohs that show that the Egyptians were aware that their culture was dependent upon the delivery of natural resources from other parts of the Earth. They did not see their existence threatened by people living upstream. The upstream riparian cultures in Sudan and in Ethiopia could have theoretically used agriculture so that a considerable portion of the Nile water would be transported back to the atmosphere through evaporation and thus could not have even reached the already densely settled Nile valley. Particularly since they often suffered hunger and famine due to drought, they could have used the Nile water and sediment for themselves. However, they were much too weak to compete with the mighty Egyptians for these valuable resources.

In principle, this is how it has been up to now. In the 1980s, Sudan and Ethiopia were hit by massive droughts. Egypt, however, was very well protected against droughts. This was because of technological measures that Egypt undertook in order to control the discharge of the Nile. To do this, a dam was built near the city of Aswan in 1902 and the height was raised in 1912 and again in 1933. The lake that was created was not very big, but sufficed so that the discharge of the Nile no longer dropped below 550 m³/s during the dry season. This discharge was ensured by damming the water during the rainy season at the end of August and then releasing it in the dry season during April and May. The dam was too small to hold back the entire flood wave of the Nile. Therefore, the first part of the flood wave in June, July, and the beginning of August was diverted around the dam. Not until the end of the rainy season at the end of August was the dam allowed to fill. Thus, especially at the beginning of the rainy season, the valuable fertile silt transported by the Nile reached the farmers' fields downstream. In addition, the water held back by the dam could be used to irrigate additional fields and thus grow food during the dry season. However, this additional food could not keep pace with the rapidly growing population. A new dam was needed, which would be capable of controlling the entire floodwaters of the Nile. And so the Aswan High Dam was finished in 1970, a few kilometers upstream from the old dam. This reservoir dams the Nile to form a gigantic lake, which stretches far into Sudan.

The Aswan High Dam

The Aswan High Dam and the irrigation systems from the Aral Sea region are both examples of large-scale technological projects that characterize how the 20th century handled the debate about natural resources. Many such large-scale technological projects that were planned and also carried out were characterized by a mixture of developing awareness of the problems and naive, unbroken faith in advanced technology in Russia, Europe, and the USA. It was the time of the first space flights, the first atomic reactors, and the first organ transplants. Egypt, together with Russia and America, was searching for answers to increasing population pressure in their country. Three developments at that time convinced them:

1   the effectiveness and above all the affordability of chemical fertilizers and pesticides,
2   the promising advancements in crop research, and
3   the green revolution, initiated in Asia by the World Bank, which by combining the first two developments resulted in incredible yield increases in practice.

Everyone thought that the long-desired technologies necessary to feed the masses and ensure prosperity were finally available. The idea that a dam could "tame the Nile," something that their revered ancestors had not succeeded in doing, was too tempting not continue with. At bottom, the Egyptians finally wanted independence from the extreme fluctuations in the water flow of the Nile. This would then ensure several harvests a year. Of course, they knew about the fertility of the Nile silt and its importance for agriculture in the Nile valley and that the planned dam would retain the silt almost completely. However, the introduction of chemical fertilizers in Europe, America, and Russia strengthened the Egyptians' belief that they could do without the nutrients delivered by the regular Nile floods. In the meantime, the average consumption of nitrogen, phosphorus, and potassium in Egypt has risen to a total of 372 kg per hectare per year, an immense amount.

Ultimately, near the city of Aswan, a 111-m high dam almost 4 km long was constructed, which created Lake Nasser. Today, Lake Nasser dams the Nile for 480 km, 160 km of that reaching into neighboring Sudan. The entire Abu Simbel temple complex and 90,000 people had to be relocated, which required quite an intricate procedure. The Aswan High Dam is one of the largest water projects in the world. Its size is only surpassed by the Itaipu Dam in Brazil and the Three Gorges Dam in China. In hydraulic terms, the Aswan High Dam is resoundingly successful, as shown in Fig. 15. It shows the course of the Nile discharge from 1950 to 1990. The variability of the discharge is clearly seen with peak values of up to 11,500 m³/s during the annual Nile floods and a decrease to less than 500 m³/s in dry years (e.g. around 1960) until 1965. Afterwards, the peak values decrease continually, at first due to the filling of the reservoir with floodwater. After 1968, the full effectiveness of the dam in reducing the summer floods can be clearly seen.

Can such a massive impact upon nature be evaluated purely for its usefulness for humans and its damage to nature?

In doing so, limits are reached. Such a large-scale project represents a crossroad for the regions involved. The consequences

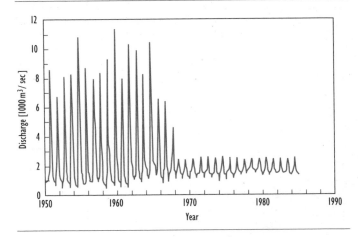

Figure 15 Discharge of the Nile near Aswan from 1950 to 1990

are generally incisive and the effects of the project upon other developmental factors, such as population growth, energy consumption, electrification, or industrialization are considerable. Due to this, it is impossible to say whether the development of the region would have been better with or without the realization of the large-scale project. Furthermore, there are no areas for comparison, which could serve as a reference, in order to test the impact of the project. However, looking back, one can definitely list positive and negative effects of the Aswan High Dam.

The Aswan High Dam has been and is extremely useful for the Egyptian economy and increasingly for the Sudanese also. With the dam, all the floodwater can be stored and water can be provided in a controlled manner when needed. Thus, enough water is available for irrigating hundreds of thousands of hectares of farmland. In addition, a flourishing fish industry has

Country	Population [million]	Population growth [%/year]	Gross per capita income [US-$]	GNP [billions of US-$]	Internal, renewable water resources [m³/person and year]
Uganda	22.0	3.0	310	6.3	1891
Tanzania	33.7	2.0	280	9.3	2773
Sudan	29.7	2.0	320	11.2	1279
Rwanda	8.5	2.0	250	1.8	833
Kenya	30.1	2.3	360	10.4	739
Ethiopia	64.0	2.0	100	6.3	2059
Eritrea	4.0	3.0	170	0.6	815
Egypt	63.8	1.8	1490	98.3	29
Congo	51.3	3.0			21,973
Burundi	6.8	2.0	110	0.7	579

Table 3 Key values of the social conditions in countries in the Nile catchment area from the year 2000 (from: Nicol, 2000).

established itself at the lake and provides the population with protein. The dam has drastically improved the navigation conditions upstream as well as downstream, in that navigable water depths, even for larger ships, are ensured year round. The dam also created enormous amounts of electricity from renewable energy. This has brought Egypt moderate prosperity compared to its neighbors, as shown in Table 3.

The fourth column in Table 3 compares the per capita gross income of the populations in the countries along the Nile. The per capita income in Egypt is clearly far above the rest. Especially striking is the difference between Ethiopia and Egypt. Both countries have populations of approximately 70 million. Ethiopia is located in the south and is relatively rich in precipitation, whereas Egypt is located in the relatively dry north. This clearly

Figure 16   Conventional irrigation technology in Egyptian agriculture. A waterwheel is used to raise groundwater for irrigation (Photo: W. Mauser)

shows the unequal distribution of the usage of the Nile water for the populations living in the various regions of the Nile.

However, the Aswan High Dam also has its drawbacks. First and foremost, the gradual decrease in the fertility of the soil in the Nile floodplains must be mentioned. This is due to the fact that almost all of the sediment load from the annual floods is held back in Lake Nasser and is therefore not available for the fields downstream. Egypt's annual chemical fertilizer consumption of one million tons nowadays is not a full-fledged substitute for the estimated 40 million tons of silt that the Nile floods left annually on the floodplain fields and in the delta.

Fig. 16 gives an impression of how, even today, conventional, energy-efficient techniques are used in the Nile valley for intensive agricultural. Water is transported to the fields either through canals from the Nile or simple machines are used to extract Nile-enriched groundwater.

Let us now take a look at other countries that share the catchment area and the waters of the Nile besides Egypt, the dominant economic force in the region. The ratio between population growth and poverty has become a determinant. If economic growth cannot keep up with population growth, the inevitable result is increased poverty in the population. This means that economic growth of at least 3% is necessary to keep up with an annual population growth of 3%, in order to absorb the increasing population into the workforce and allow funds for social development. The third column in Table 3 shows the population growth in the Nile countries. It shows that in many of the countries, the population growth is around 2.5–3%.

Considering the income differences shown in the fourth column in Table 3 and the differences in population growth shown in column three between the downstream and upstream riparian countries, it is not surprising that Egypt is closely watching Ethiopia's plans to develop its water resources. Ethiopia's plans to introduce large-scale irrigation are alarming for Egypt, because they would mean increased evaporation and transpiration in the upper course of the Nile and thus a reduction in the Nile discharge. At the present, Ethiopia is not economically able to set up a large-scale irrigation system. Its agriculture is almost completely dependent upon the annual changing precipitation. In the future, this can and must change, otherwise Ethiopia will not be able to feed its growing population.

On the other hand, the availability and amount of renewable (excluding the deep groundwater that is thousands of years old) water resources in these countries, as compared to Egypt, is quite positive, as clearly shown in the sixth column of Table 3. In these terms, Egypt is by far the last of the Nile countries, with 29 m³ water per person per year. Ethiopia, with available renewable water resources of 2059 m³ per person per year, has far more. Ethiopia can thus be considered to have good potential to develop independent, sustainable water-resources management. However, almost all development options to ensure food security for the population in the upper reaches of the Nile will have a negative impact upon Egypt's available water resources. This represents a latent conflict that has been smoldering for years between the Nile countries. It is a typical upstream/downstream conflict about natural resources. The conflict will intensify in the coming years. Although the irrigation regions have been widely extended and thus also the agricultural production, natural limits are being reached. Even though Egypt has created the necessary technical prerequisites by building the Aswan High Dam and, based on the imported water resources and very intensive agriculture, is harvesting three times a year, the present available amount of water in Egypt is not sufficient to produce the necessary food for the population. Two other factors limit the further intensification of the agriculture: 1) Egypt is already using 98% of the available water resources. 2) Egypt is unable to easily extend the crop area in the Nile delta or in the Nile valley any further.

Cereals, including millet, are the most important crop in Egypt. In 2002, about a million hectares of cereals were irrigated. To do this, 5.3 km³ water was used. That is almost 10% of the entire amount of water that is available in Egypt for irrigation (Mason, 2004). However, the amount of cereals produced was not enough to be self-sufficient. For this, 1.7 million hectares of cropland would be necessary. Self-sufficiency is an important political goal in the Nile countries. It is not uncommon to pursue self-sufficiency even against economic rationale. The self-sufficiency rate, i.e. the percentage of cereals grown versus cereals consumed in Egypt, has risen from 25% in 1982 to 60% in 2000, due to extending the irrigation areas. This was achieved by linking the price of Egyptian cereals from 1982 to 1994 to the price on the world market, which led to a price increase. However, the self-sufficiency rate did not increase to 100%. At present, Egypt still imports 40% of its needed cereals. Even if the self-sufficiency rate for cereals were to be achieved, this could only happen at the cost of other crops, which would then not have enough water for irrigation. Thus, due to the limited water resources, agriculture in Egypt becomes a zero-sum game.

National, unilateral approaches, especially due to the limited economic power of the countries involved, help very little here. Eight of the ten countries are LCDs (Least Developed Countries) or Fourth World countries. What are the challenges that confront all of the Nile countries? The following conflict chain can be recognized:

1   A limited amount of water is used by a population that annually grows by 2–3%. However, a simultaneous increase in the efficiency of water consumption does not go hand-in-hand with the growth of the population. Thus, water becomes continually scarcer.

2   The downstream riparian countries are concerned about a decrease in the water supply due to the observed developments in water consumption by the upstream riparian countries.

3   At the same time, the upstream riparian countries are concerned that the downstream riparian countries could stunt their development.

4   There are socio-economical and political limits to the

capability of the Nile countries in finding alternatives to the present trends in water consumption.

5. There is no treaty on water allocation that is accepted by all the Nile countries. Egypt and Sudan insist upon "traditional rights" and the validity of a 1959 treaty that they signed. The upstream riparian countries want a new Nile water treaty.

6. There have already been isolated, apprehensive claims of diplomatic tension and downright threats between the Nile countries, in particular between Egypt and Ethiopia.

7. Through this, and due to disunity between the Nile countries, international water-related investments are blocked.

At the end of this book, we will return to the catchment area of the Nile, when I report on the routes that the involved countries could take together to try and resolve the apparent conflicts about the water resources of the Nile peacefully and cooperatively.

But first, I would like to deal more closely with the issues that are necessary for a deeper understanding of the Nile case study, and that are a central topic of this book.

4 How Much Water is Available? — A New Perspective

In Chapter 2, I emphasized the central role water plays in the functioning of Earth's life-support system and thus for human survival. We became acquainted with the planet as a complicated system of interrelated processes. It became clear that life on Earth is dependent upon an intact water cycle and that this dependency creates vital goods and services.

In Chapter 3, I presented two case studies that showed on the one hand to what degree humans are now capable of controlling the water cycle and on the other hand of changing water flow. Both cases dealt with large-scale transformation of blue water into green water. The reasons for carrying out these interventions in both cases had to do with supplying a growing population with food and agricultural raw materials.

Due to problems apparent in large-scale projects, worries about the impact upon natural cycles, especially the water cycle, due to the steadily increasing world population, have increased in the last thirty to forty years. Many people have formed the opinion that the world is facing acute water shortages or is at least afflicted by serious water problems. In the next chapter, I will deal with the issue of how opinion concerning the aforementioned problems has changed over time and what findings led to this.

In the 1970s, the main concern was with the supply of drinking water. Rightly so, the public became aware that large parts of the world's population did not have access to safe, i.e. available and clean, drinking water, some even to this day. In many regions, drinking water was (and is) the primary source of pathogenic germs. Therefore, the drinking-water problem was seen first and foremost as a health problem hampering the development of the regions affected. The first UN "Water Conference" in 1977 in Mar del Plata, Argentina, addressed these concerns for the first time and laid the foundation for the ensuing first International Decade for Clean Drinking Water from 1981 to 1990. Its aim was to ensure access to clean drinking water across the world within the decade, as well as to significantly improve health and sanitation conditions for the world's population. As we now know, those goals were only partially achieved. It is even often said that the programs that were begun were completely useless. This was certainly not because the programs were not active; they were financially well-endowed. After all, they were the first programs that brought experts from all countries together peacefully and promised to use international solidarity to eradicate blatant and evident grievances. This vision inspired and motivated the most dedicated and qualified experts of their generation, as is happening similarly today in genetics in trying to eradicate diseases.

What was the reason for its only partial success? Were we looking for solutions in the wrong places? Was the problem too narrowly defined? Or was our knowledge about the relationship between humans and water too limited?

In the meantime, the world has widened its knowledge. At first, the programs were only set up to master the technical problems related to drinking water and hygiene problems. However, it was soon clear that although technology is a prerequisite for these solutions, they need an appropriate social environment in order to be effective. Technologies must be applied and maintained daily for them to be effective. They need an infrastructure with knowledge and capital in order to be used and maintained. These prerequisites were (and are) not available in impoverished regions. Furthermore, it was finally recognized that it was the sources of the drinking water that were causing the actual problems. Due to extensive pollution of these sources and damage to the ecosystem due to overgrazing, intensification of agriculture, and increasing population density, the ecosystem could no longer provide sufficiently clean water. Thus, considering the poverty of the population concerned, the technological solutions failed.

As a result, the international programs began to carry out surveys on both regional and global levels, based on different countries, as to how much water is used by humans. The goal was to find out how much blue water is already used and what level of water reserves are still available. The findings were that water use by humans is generally high and that it is directly and closely coupled with population growth worldwide. This was not initially recognized. However, these investigations usually had a decisive flaw: they did not take multiple uses of water into consideration.

4.1 The Dublin statement on water and sustainable development

During the course of the UN Conference on Environment and Development in 1992 in Rio de Janeiro (also known as the "Earth Summit" or "Rio Conference") the Dublin Statement on water use was developed (see box, page 67ff.). This was a radical change from previous thinking and opened new perspectives on water use. The Dublin Statement is guided by the notion that worldwide water use must be based upon an integrated approach that includes humans and nature, water and land resources. It formulates basic human rights for water and hygiene and rightly emphasizes the central role that women play in improving these conditions. For the first time, the Dublin Statement dealt with the core topics of "sustainable development" and "water." Furthermore, the statement also addressed how these goals should be achieved: in a participatory manner, in which all stakeholders are included in the solution to the problem as well as in the decisions and their implementation. This was revolutionary for many countries – not just the dictatorships in Africa, the Near East, and Latin America, but also venerable democracies in Europe with slow-moving bureaucracies. This approach does not comply with the perception nor the common practice used hitherto to solve complex problems.

"In commending this Dublin Statement to the world leaders assembled at the United Nations Conference on Environment and Development (UNCED) in Rio de Janeiro in June 1992, the Conference participants urge all governments to study carefully the specific activities and means of implementation recommended in the Conference Report, and to translate those recommendations into urgent action programmes for Water and Sustainable Development

Guiding principles

Concerted action is needed to reverse the present trends of overconsumption, pollution, and rising threats from drought and floods. The Conference Report sets out recommendations for action at local, national and international levels, based on four guiding principles.

Principle No. 1 — Fresh water is a finite and vulnerable resource, essential to sustain life, development and the environment

Since water sustains life, effective management of water resources demands a holistic approach, linking social and economic development with protection of natural ecosystems. Effective management links land and water uses across the whole of a catchment area or groundwater aquifer.

Principle No. 2 — Water development and management should be based on a participatory approach, involving users, planners and policy-makers at all levels

The participatory approach involves raising awareness of the importance of water among policy-makers and the general public. It means that decisions are taken at the lowest appropriate level, with full public consultation and involvement of users in the planning and implementation of water projects.

Principle No. 3 — Women play a central part in the provision, management and safeguarding of water

This pivotal role of women as providers and users of water and guardians of the living environment has seldom been reflected in institutional arrangements for the development and management of water resources. Acceptance and implementation of this principle requires positive policies to address women's specific needs and to equip and empower women to participate at all levels in water resources programmes, including decision-making and implementation, in ways defined by them.

Principle No. 4 — Water has an economic value in all its competing uses and should be recognized as an economic good

Within this principle, it is vital to recognize first the basic right of all human beings to have access to clean water and sanitation at an affordable price. Past failure to recognize the economic value of water has led to wasteful and environmentally damaging uses of the resource. Managing water as an economic good is an important way of achieving efficient and equitable use, and of encouraging conservation and protection of water resources."

The Dublin Statement vividly shows how far the experts have come in the thirty years since the first technology-driven programs for improving the planet's water situation. The guiding principles of the Dublin Statement were confirmed in the Rio Conference in 1992. However, the challenge to view water as an economic good triggered an intense controversy, which continues to this day. Many attribute this concept to neo-liberal thinking, which judges anything and everything in economic terms. This is at odds with the views that many cultures have with regard to water. Water is considered holy in all of the old cultures. However, generally this did not ensure that water was treated with awe or respect. In these cultures, water was often treated as a religious good, simply because it could not be bought or sold.

It is a shame that it is not an automatic social responsibility to provide everyone with a clean water supply or better yet to ensure that no one pollutes water, even with its sacred status in these cultures. Since it has no owner and thus ownership cannot change, there is no incentive in these cultures to use water sparingly or carefully. This does not help the poor. The cultures involved claim that the commodification of water resources would particularly affect the poorest parts of the population and is thus anti-social. This discussion and its obvious inconsistencies are typical of the worldwide debate about the Dublin Statement and show how far water has moved away from the purely technological issue of water supply.

At the second world water forum in 2000, the vague predictions of the future developments of the worldwide water situation were announced, as mentioned at the beginning of this book (Cosgrove and Rijsberman, 2000). In the meantime, also because of the continuing and increasingly intense discussion on climate change, thorough investigations were carried out into possible further developments of water resources. In doing so, the development of the world population and changes in climate were investigated with an integrated approach, as demanded in the Dublin Statement. The result of these integrated studies is that mankind inevitably faces serious water scarcity, due to population pressures, general decline in water quality, climate change, and the non-sustainable management of water resources.

It has become absolutely clear that despite the advances made in water supply and hygiene in the past thirty years, one billion people still do not have access to adequate drinking water and 2.8 billion do not have access to sufficient sanitation. It is upsetting and alarming that even after all the work put forth in the last thirty years of the 20th century that there are still millions of women and children in developing countries who are forced to collect untreated water from various suspect sources, which are often so far away that they spend the better part of their life collecting that water.

Later on, I will come back to the fact that the frustration and unhappiness about these conditions are not due to an actual shortage of water on Earth, but rather due to the unsustainable management of water resources.

In the meantime, it has become obvious that the continual and increasing water use by humans has a profound impact upon the planet's ecosystems. In addition, there is growing understanding that sustainable management of water reserves can only be achieved if water for humans and water for nature are considered together.

The system analysis provided in Chapter 2 showed the different functions of water on Earth. These considerations can now be used to understand the role that water plays for humans and nature. What does a new appraisal of Earth's water resources look like, if the belief that water is a resource that solely exists to satisfy human wants and needs and that its availability is purely a question of correct technologies is no longer held?

This new survey cannot alter the map of precipitation on Earth as shown in Fig. 7. It remains the starting point and limiting factor for all other considerations. However, the new survey has to ask new questions. From the standpoint of Earth's life-support system on Earth, what actually is a water resource? What do we actually mean when we say "human pressure upon water resources?" What produces this pressure? Have we considered the fact in the previous concepts of water scarcity and water availability that water is needed to maintain vital ecosystem-services and that therefore both nature and humans need the same resource?

However, first we should look at how much water is involved in the turnover on the continents and through which mechanisms, both large and small, humans are involved in the turnover.

4.2 Water in numbers

A total of 113,500 km³ precipitation falls annually on the surface of the Earth. This corresponds to a cube with edges of over 48 km. At first, this appears to be an unimaginable amount of water. This cube of water could fill about 750 billion bathtubs (of 150 liters). At the current world population of 6.5 billion people, this would be 320 filled bathtubs per person per day. This is certainly more than anyone needs to bathe and also more than anyone could possibly imagine needing per day. However, as we will see in the discussion of this topic, this amount is quickly put into perspective.

Compared to the total amount of fresh water on Earth, 35 billion km³, another unimaginably large amount, the annual amount of precipitation is minuscule. This is only 3.2 per mill of the entire amount of fresh water. If 3.2 per mill of the entire amount of fresh water is replaced every year by precipitation, then on average, mathematically at least, it takes 300 years for the entire amount of fresh water to be exchanged once. Most of the fresh water, namely more than 60%, is stored in the, currently still large, glaciers of the Antarctic. Some 6% is in the glaciers of Greenland and 30% is locked in geological layers and makes up the deep groundwater. Thus, 96% of the reserves of fresh water cannot be tapped for tens of thousands of years.

This means that only 3 per mill of the entire amount of fresh water on Earth is stored in our familiar lakes, rivers, bogs, and swamps as well as in the soil. This water is very mobile, compared to the water in the glaciers and the groundwater. The amount of annual precipitation and the amount of mobile, near-surface water are approximately equal in amount, approximately 3 per mill of the entire amount. This is confirmed by farmers who experience the annual turnover of water resources in the rhythm of the seasons during the course of a year. Even though

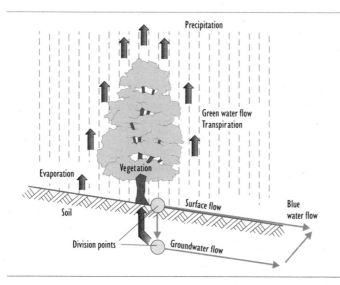

Figure 17 Division of precipitation into blue and green water flow

the annual precipitation only makes up 3 per mill of the entire amount of fresh water, it is the basis of our life.

The precipitation creates the blue water flow in the rivers, lakes, and groundwater bodies. It transports 42,650 km³ annually and with this, about a third of the entire 113,500 km³ of precipitation into the oceans. The rest of the water flow is made up of water vapor, which flows back into the atmosphere as evaporation from the surface of the Earth. Annually, some 70,850 km³ of water moves from the Earth's surface back into the atmosphere as evaporation. Thus, the green water flow is approximately twice the size of the blue water flow. Two-thirds of the precipitation on the Earth's surface becomes green water. Thus, if we consider the water resources in streams, rivers, and groundwater, we are considering the lesser part.

The ratio of blue to green water determines the percentage of precipitation that is available for evaporation and thus can be used for plant growth. However, it also determines the percentage of precipitation that feeds the rivers and thus can be used for hydroelectric power and navigation. The stated values are averages for all areas of land and include deserts as well as wetlands and cities. Regionally, the division of the precipitation into blue and green water varies greatly. What factors determine this division?

Fig. 17 schematically shows the division of precipitation into blue and green water. When precipitation falls on the Earth, part of it seeps into the ground and part of it forms puddles on the surface or flows as surface flow. This is the first division of precipitation. This is where it is determined how much water seeps into the ground and thus how much water is available for vegetation as moisture in the soil. A second division occurs in the soil itself. The root density of the vegetation determines how much green water is taken out of the soil by the plants and transported into the atmosphere. Water that is not used by the vegetation seeps into the groundwater and flows in the soil and groundwater as slow water flow to the nearest stream or river.

Both of these division points are forks in the road that direct the water flow from the precipitation into irrevocably different paths and thus further different paths through the Earth system. The surface flow and the groundwater flow unite to form the blue water flow and the evaporation from the surface and the transpiration of vegetation unite to form the green water flow.

5 Water and Land Use

5.1 What do people do locally?

A decisive factor for the determination of the further paths that water takes, therefore, is what exactly happens at the dividing points. That is, it is possible to influence these forks in the road by setting up obstacles to direct the water flow in one direction or another? The first point of division can be influenced in favor of, or to the disadvantage of, the blue or green water through surface compaction, soil erosion, forest clearing, i.e. through all types of land-use changes. This can take on drastic proportions as seen in Fig. 18 with the example of a clear-cut in the Harz Mountains in Germany.

On the left-hand side of Fig. 18, two small forest catchment areas are schematically shown. They are in the Harz Mountains and they both were originally covered with coniferous forests and are only 1.5 km apart. This ensures that both areas receive the same amount of precipitation. Since the forest management planned a clear-cut with reforestation in one of the forests for 1957, measuring instruments were set up in both areas in 1955. Thus, in the summer of 1955, the effects of a storm upon the discharge could be observed for both areas. The results of these observations are shown on the right-hand side of Fig. 18. Both catchment areas reacted almost identically to the storm. Approximately one hour after the start of the precipitation,

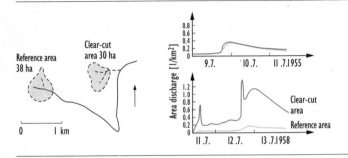

Figure 18 Change in the division of the precipitation into blue and green
water with the example of a forest clearing in the Harz
Mountains in Germany in the 1950s

the discharge rose sharply and then normalized within two
days. The curves clearly show how at first the precipitation is
absorbed by the soil and then slowly travels through the soil
and within two days is continually released by the soil to the
surface water. Three years later, after one area had been clear-
cut in 1957, another summer storm occurred on two consecutive
days over both catchment areas. The results of the observations
can be seen in the bottom right of the graph. The forested area
reacted similarly to the event three years earlier. In the clear-cut
area, however, the division of the precipitation into blue and
green water was radically differently. If the discharge curves for
the clear-cut area and the natural area are compared, two things
are obvious:

1   The discharge curve from the clear-cut area shows, as
    compared to the natural area, distinct, steep and short
    discharge peaks. These are the result of massive changes at the
    first division point. A large part of the soil has no vegetation

cover, the tree roots are gone and thus less precipitation can enter the soil and the faster surface flow increases.

2 The amount of water that leaves the catchment area as discharge after the storm is greatly increased as compared to the natural area. This is a result of the massive change at the second division point. Since the vegetation is gone, the water no longer evaporates into the atmosphere as green water flow.

As a consequence, the amount of water that flows through the soil into the surface water is significantly larger. If the course of the curves is examined closely, it can be seen how the soil reacts relatively slowly on the first day of the storm and stores the precipitation to some extent, releasing very little additional water. On the second day, it can be clearly seen how the soil fills with water during the course of the storm and releases it in a peaked and tapered-off curve.

Obviously, processes occurring at the two division points determine the fate of the precipitation. Whereas in 1955, a large part of the precipitation was stored and went through the vegetation, in 1958 the greater part of the precipitation left the catchment area as surface flow or after a brief passage through the soil. In addition, there is a strong acceleration of the discharge, because the trees that acted as obstacles to the water flow are gone. Thus, the precipitation was only available for use as blue water for a short time.

This small example clearly shows where people intervene in the water cycle. To a considerable degree, it is land-use decisions that determine the water dynamics on the surface of the land. Land use has a strong effect upon the two key division points between blue and green water, namely on the surface and in the soil. Thus land use modifies the entire water cycle. Every change

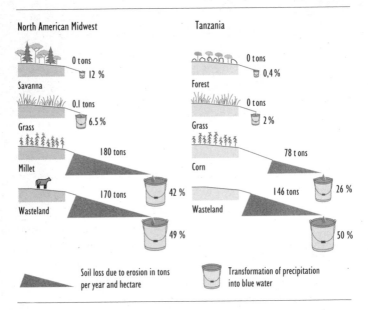

Figure 19 Results of investigations on the influence of land use on the division of the precipitation into blue and green water flow as well as the amount of eroded material in tons per hectare in the American Midwest and in Tanzania (after Rapp, 1972)

in the type of vegetation, plant type or cultivation changes the partitioning between blue and green water.

This first example was taken from forestry and shows the serious effects that land-use changes can have upon the local water balance. Just as important worldwide, if not more important, are changes in the land surface due to the introduction, development, and expansion of agriculture.

Fig. 19 shows the drastic change in the blue water flow due to changes in land use in two different regions. The left shows the development of a forested area in the American Midwest after the settlement in the 19th century. At first the forest was cleared and the area used as pasture, then corn was cultivated and now the area, since it is wasteland, is only used for limited pasturing. Whereas only 12% of the precipitation left the original forest as blue water and 88% entered the atmosphere as green water via evaporation, this value decreases when the area is clear-cut. However, the subsequent cultivation of corn lets the amount of precipitation which becomes blue water increase to 42%. The following degradation to wasteland increases the amount even further to 49%. This transformation goes hand-in-hand with a massive increase in erosion, which is usually insignificant in forests. With grass, the erosion increases to 100 kg per hectare per year and reaches 180 tons for corn and 170 tons for wasteland. A similar picture results if the consequences of man-made impacts upon the water balance in a very different region of the world are considered. The right-hand column of Fig. 19 shows the transformation of savanna to fallow via clearing, grassland, and millet cultivation in Tanzania. Due to the tropical climate, the dominant savanna is capable of evaporating 99.6% of the precipitation leaving almost no water for the blue water flow. With grass, this value decreases to 98%. Not until its transformation to farmland and the introduction of millet as a crop does the blue water flow increase to 26% of the precipitation. The wasteland that is left behind after the destruction of the land due to the millet crops and the resulting erosion does not react very differently in tropical Tanzania than in the temperate American Midwest. Here also, large amounts of the soil material is transported away by the surface flow and is thus lost for further agricultural use.

The examples show again very keenly the crucial importance that both division points, shown in Fig. 17, have and the importance of vegetation for the further use of precipitation. The first point of division determines the amount of water that seeps into the soil. Through several factors, the vegetation influences this infiltration and thus the amount of surface flow. Investigations of different plant types and ecosystems have shown that root length and the density of the root network, the leaf area of the vegetation, the amount of leaves that fall as litter to the ground, as well as the vegetation's microbiological impact are the most important factors for the capacity of the surface of the soil to absorb precipitation.

At the second division point, soil, vegetation, and climate have complex interactions, which determine the division between the green water flow and the subsurface blue water flow. Here, the roots, with their capacity to loosen the soil and absorb water, are also a decisive factor for the further flow of the water out of the soil. As can be seen in Fig. 19, energy input, temperature, and humidity are also important factors that climatically regulate the amount of evaporation. It is the high transpiration of the savanna in tropical Tanzania which evaporates more than 99% of the precipitation. This value is not achieved in the USA for climatic reasons. The number of precipitation events and thus the number of soaking and drying cycles of the soil surface and leaves through precipitation is similarly important for the unproductive green water flow, i.e. the evaporation from the ground and leaf surfaces, as the shading of the soil by the vegetation. Through surface evaporation, which occurs during every rainfall and does not contribute to plant growth, valuable precipitation is unproductively lost.

Besides physical and biological factors, which work at both points of division, and determine the transport paths of the water through the biosphere, the agricultural practices of farmers have a decisive impact upon the division. To a high degree, the surface treatment of the soil through plowing, harrowing, tilling, mulching, and rotating crops determines the capacity of agricultural soils to absorb precipitation and thus the behavior of the first division point. Unsuitable plowing under very wet conditions and with heavy machinery leads to compaction of the soil and reduces the amount of precipitation is absorbed in it by up to 90%. This leads to a corresponding increase in the surface flow due to incorrectly plowed fields. If the soil is too tightly compacted, the roots cannot penetrate it, which has a negative effect upon nutrient supply and plant growth.

At the second division point, above all, the farmer has an impact through yield management. Correct crop selection, fertilization, and pest control ensure that the plants grow roots and leaves optimally and thus regulate the transpiration optimally. In this case, the plants can utilize the water resources available in the soil to their fullest extent.

In the tropical savannas of Africa with the often long dry periods and short rainy seasons, the unproductive green water flow of the evaporation from the surface after the short but heavy precipitation is often the dominant part of the water flow. This is because under these natural conditions, there is not enough precipitation to ensure an adequate supply for vegetation cover, so that it can ripen and produce seeds, and vegetation cover does not form. Thus, evaporation is quicker than transpiration in these regions and "snatches" the water away from the vegetation. To reduce the unproductive green water flow from the surface here, agricultural practices should be chosen that change the microclimate directly at the surface, so that evaporation is reduced and the plants have a chance to use the infiltrating water for transpiration. A prime example of this is covering the surface with mulch. However, also plowing the surface soil under, after it has been soaked by a precipitation event, hinders the immediate evaporation of the rainwater.

As Fig. 19 indicates, the mechanisms described are universally applicable in the division of precipitation into blue and green water flows. In principle they do not change from country to country or from climate region to climate region. The dividing mechanisms and forks in the paths are also valid at all levels. They influence the growing conditions of the individual plants, home-cultivated front yards, the small farms in China with areas of tenths of a hectare, the large-scale farms in the USA, in Canada, Brazil, or East Germany, with fields that are up to several thousand hectares and, last but not least, entire river catchment areas with hundred of thousands to millions of square kilometers. Humans have a massive impact upon the availability of water through these and the choice of land use.

An extreme, and if it were not so grave for the people involved, very odd example of change in water availability is the Cherrapunji region in India. Cherrapunji is in the humid tropics and is often called the "wettest desert on Earth." The amount of precipitation in the region, 11,400 mm annually, is very abundant, some twelve times that which falls in Germany. Despite this, the region suffers from massive water shortages. Why? The reasons lie in the large variation in the annual precipitation. A distinct dry season, in which the population is dependent upon stored water, is followed by a very intensive rainy season, during which the population could fill all of the reservoirs with ease. However, due to man's almost complete destruction of the landscape, almost all of the natural reservoirs are gone. In particular, the clear-cutting of the original forests has exposed the land in the entire area to the intensive tropical precipitation. The result was a dramatic change in the behavior of the first point of division in the topsoil. It changed, as shown in Fig. 18, from a high percentage of infiltration to predominantly surface flow. This discharge creates more erosion, until the original topsoil is eroded away and the surface is reduced to uncovered bedrock, at least on the slopes. Thus the land has lost its ability to store water. In the rainy season, precipitation flows away so quickly as torrents of blue water that it is impossible to use or store the water with the infrastructure available. The water is gone. Thus, without available water, the region, despite the high amounts of precipitation, becomes a desert for its people. Only through replacing the originally abundantly-available soil reservoir by building large reservoirs such as dams and impounding reservoirs could the situation possibly be stabilized again and the soil revitalized through long-term reforestation and agricultural programs. However, there is no sign of the required funding being forthcoming.

5.2 What do people do globally?

In the last section, we focused on considerations concerning the division of water into blue and green water flow at selected sites on the surface and in the soil. It became clear, at least in principle, how and where man-made impacts can change the water cycle and achieve large effects apparently with comparatively little effort. The mechanisms described fit in the picture shown in the examples of the large-scale hydraulic projects of Aral Sea and the Nile catchment area. In both cases, the purpose of the hydraulic works was the redirection of the natural water flow towards more green water.

The key to understanding the man-made strain upon the water cycle and thus the entire life-support system is the clarification of the coupling between the green and blue water flow, mankind's motives for the redirection of the flow, and the value of the products obtained. After all, these dynamic changes were not carried out just for fun, but rather were necessary to ensure the survival of a large population.

At this point, fundamental questions arise that go beyond the case studies and the selected considerations about the division of precipitation. What was the original, natural, blue and green water flow on Earth like? What is the relationship between green water flow and land use, which ensures our food supply through agriculture? What do we receive for managing the blue and green water flow in terms of food products? After all, for the most part, the massive redirection carried out in the examples given, the Aral Sea and the Nile, were made with massive investments. How did the worldwide change in land use occur and what are our future options?

This is a lot of questions. They lead us back to the close coupling of the water and carbon cycles, which is a characteristic feature of the Earth and which we dealt with in Chapter 2 in terms of the planet's life-support system. Now, let us consider this coupling from a human viewpoint! Humans learned to understand and use this coupling very early in the course of their development. It is the basis for our agriculture, i.e. the targeted production of biomass beyond natural productivity. In addition to modifying plants through breeding, humans in particular learned to use water strategically and purposefully.

This is based on a simple but fundamental relationship. The net primary production of plants, i.e. the amount of carbon that the plants take in out of the atmosphere and use to produce biomass, is directly and approximately linearly coupled with the green water flow through the plant. This is true in nature as well as in cases brought about by man. An increase in plant biomass production, which may occur for instance because of increased solar radiation, more favorable temperatures, or a prolonged growth period has always led to a corresponding increase in the green water flow through the plants.

As shown in Fig. 8, the stomata in the leaves allow the gas

Transpiration coefficient [l/kg dry mass]		Transpiration coefficient [l/kg dry mass]	
C3-plants		Deciduous trees	
Rice	680	Oak	340
Rye	630	Birch	320
Wheat	540	Beech	170
Barley	520		
Potato	640	Conifers	
Sunflower	600	Pine	300
C4-plants		Larch	260
Corn	370	Spruce	230
Millet	300	Douglas fir	170

Table 4 Reference values for transpiration coefficients (1/kg dry mass) of selected plants and crops. The values can vary according to location.

exchange with the atmosphere and also, if CO_2 is assimilated, release water vapor at the same time. If the stomata are closed, there is no green water flow and CO_2 cannot be assimilated. Thus, plant growth ceases. Conversely, when the stomata are opened for CO_2-assimilation and thus growth, inevitably green evaporation water flows out of the leaves. Since the assimilation of CO_2 and the release of water vapor use the same leaf opening, it is unsurprising that both flows are closely coupled.

This close connection between both flows is expressed in the transpiration coefficient. It indicates how many liters of green water are used by a plant for transpiration in order to create 1 kg of dry biomass.

Table 4 shows the transpiration coefficients for selected plants. The values are differentiated for cultivated C3- and C4-plants, and deciduous and coniferous trees. C3- and C4-plants differ mainly in the way they produce dry biomass through photosynthesis of CO_2 and water. The transpired amount of water needed to produce 1 kg of dry biomass, ranges between 500 and 800 liters for the C3 crops listed in the left column. The right-hand column shows that deciduous trees as well as conifers transpire between 170 and 340 liters of water in order to create 1 kg of dry mass. The ratios are similar for the C4-plants such as corn and millet, which have transpiration coefficients around 300 l/kg dry mass.

Table 4 demonstrates the important fact that a surprisingly large amount of water is needed to produce biomass. For example, in order to produce 1 kg of dry biomass, and thus to harvest about 750 g of CO_2 out of the atmosphere, pine trees have to extract the equivalent of two full bathtubs of water (each of around 150 liters) from the soil and move it into the atmosphere. Furthermore, if we look at Table 4, we see that the green water flow required to produce 1 kg of dry mass for most crops (except for C4-plants) is more than twice that for the forests. Thus, forests are significantly more efficient CO_2-controllers than grasslands or most agricultural areas.

Converting forests to either grassland or farmland, changes the ratio between water consumption and CO_2-uptake from the atmosphere. The water vapor that enters the atmosphere through transpiration and the CO_2 that is removed from the atmosphere through photosynthesis are both greenhouse gases. Thus, in order to maintain its vital functions and for its growth, the vegetation removes a greenhouse gas (CO_2) from the atmosphere, and releases another (H_2O), balancing the concentrations of both gases in the atmosphere. Thus, the regulatory circuit of the Earth system keeps the planet's temperature in a vegetation-friendly range. At this point, we are at the junction of the coupling of the water and carbon cycles, which is a characteristic feature of the Earth.

How have humans utilized this junction between the carbon and water cycles?

Vegetation on Earth developed slowly and has changed time and again. The original distribution of vegetation on the planet slowly adapted to continuously changing precipitation, temperature, and soil conditions. It provided only a small number of animals and later humans with sufficient food for survival. Neither in the pristine swamps and forests of Central Europe, nor the savanna areas of Africa nor the wet tropical regions of Asia was the original vegetation lush enough to support more than one person per square kilometer. An increase in population density was only possible after the purposeful alteration of the natural vegetation into more nourishing plants. The transition of human cultures from simply gathering food to purposefully producing food, as described by Hahlbrock in his book *Feeding the Planet: Environmental Protection through Sustainable Agriculture* (Hahlbrock, 2007), was thus inevitably connected to a change in the composition of the vegetation. This occurred mainly through converting forests into so-called cultivated land as well as developing arid areas through irrigation. With the help of the crop types grown on the tilled land, much more food could be grown per square kilometer than before and thus nothing stood in the way of a flourishing, exponential proliferation of the human race.

However, the conversion of forests into cultivated land had consequences for the Earth system. As shown in Table 4, the correlation between the carbon and the water cycle therefore shifts. In order to remove the same amount of CO_2 from the atmosphere, the C3-grain crops need twice the amount of water as a forest does. Therefore, land use changes, principally the conversion of forests into cultivated land, are not neutral with respect to the regulation of greenhouse-gas concentrations. Since humans change the land use in order to produce food to survive, they influence the integrity of the planet's life-support system.

Now, it could be said that nature has always changed the

composition of the vegetation on Earth, long before humans even existed. So, why shouldn't humans, as part of nature, not do the same? At first, this viewpoint seems quite legitimate. However, the natural changes in vegetation differ in a decisive way from those changes that humans cause. Changes created through nature and humans have different goals. Therefore, humanity should only make changes with extreme caution.

The development of the natural vegetation distribution on Earth tells a story of the continual adaptation of plant as a consequence of natural environmental changes. They occurred due to the ice ages and interstadials, meteorite impacts, or volcanic eruptions. The adaptation itself led to new environmental conditions, to which the vegetation once again adapted. Thus, a natural regulation mechanism, which apparently works so astoundingly well that in spite of all the external influences, which have in some cases have been serious, the Earth as a whole has never left the third state of equilibrium, which is regulated by life, in the last three billion years (see Fig. 5). Natural changes in the vegetation cover of the Earth, as well as changes in its functional species composition served to stabilize life on Earth. The planet's natural vegetation seemingly "knows" by itself how it needs to react to external influences in order to stabilize itself and the Earth and thus survive.

The goals of man-made changes in land use have been totally different. They were and are primarily targeted towards increasing the population instead of maintaining the third state of equilibrium. The necessary increase in food production which extended far beyond the pre-industrial level was not provided by the Earth system "voluntarily." This increase was not a part of the genetic program of the natural plants. The increase in yield was and is laboriously wrung from nature. Thus it is not a surprise that this process resulted in a large-scale restructuring of nature. This process was vastly successful in the course of centuries of human development, by combining the targeted breeding of high-yield plants, the invention of artificial fertilizers and pesticides, and by massive restructuring of the planet's vegetation.

Therefore, man-made changes in land use are obviously not part of nature's life-sustaining regulatory cycle, which has kept the Earth in the third state of equilibrium for such a long time. These changes are fundamentally different from natural adaptations due to environmental changes.

5.3 How have people changed global land use?

Intensive study and reconstructions of worldwide human activities of the last 300 years have answered this question quite comprehensively. The development is summarized in Fig. 20.

Fig. 20 shows the changes in the major land-use categories of farmland, pastures, forests, and "other" in the last 300 years. This graph depicts farmland and pastures as land dominated by man, and forests and "other" are considered to be natural land. Deserts, bodies of water, bogs, natural grasslands, ice, as well as natural montane wastelands are included in "other." Most striking in Fig. 20 is the marked shift between the categories of "human-dominated land" and "natural land." Around 1700, the percentage of the land area that was dominated by man was under 10%. Today, this amount is around 40%.

The amount of farmland, and above all pasture, has increased in the past century. This occurred mainly at the expense of forests, which were reduced from 45% to 25%, but also at the expense of the "other" category. Above all, the percentage of natural grassland has been reduced by the expansion of pasture from 48% then to 35% now. What led to this?

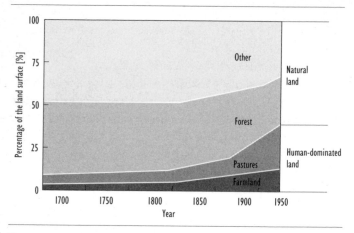

Figure 20 Worldwide changes in land use since 1700 (from
Geographie, 2007, after Steffen, 2004)

By domesticating livestock, establishing agriculture, and
developing irrigation methods, humans had three instruments
available with which they could effect land-use changes. As a
result, they moved forward in three different directions.

5.4 People were nomads

One approach was to utilize the arid areas on Earth more intensively, above all the desert margins. In these savanna and steppe
regions, which include the northern Sahel in Africa, large parts
of the southern Midwest and the West of the USA, the broad
grasslands of South America, and large areas in northern China,
the precipitation is too low and too irregular to support permanent agriculture. In these areas, the vegetation grows only

sparsely and there is often no closed vegetation cover. Thus, there are large open spaces between the plants. Due to the shortage of water, the vegetation grows slowly and develops a high percentage of cellulose, and in particular lignin which serves to support and stabilize the plants in dry periods.

Domesticated animals, and also wild ones, make up the bulk of the food supply for populations living in arid areas on Earth. All of these animals have a capability that humans do not have: the ability to digest cellulose, which is an important constituent of the vegetation in arid areas. Humans cannot digest cellulose and so it has no calorific value for them; it is considered as dietary fiber in the human food supply. Therefore, humans living in these arid regions can only utilize a small part of the sparsely growing vegetation. Thus, the limits for gathering enough food daily are quickly reached, especially with decreasing precipitation at the edge of the deserts. Besides the inability to digest cellulose, humans suffer under a second handicap. As bipeds who walk upright, they are not able to cover large areas at high speeds, while simultaneously grazing the vegetation. Therefore, the amount of calories needed as food to cover the daily energy demand of at least 2500 kcal per day, must be available within a relatively small area of about 3 km or within forty-five minutes of where they live so that they are able to gather that food in the course of a day. Furthermore, the food should contain the least amount of cellulose and the largest possible amount of carbohydrates and protein. A minimum of 500 mm annual precipitation is necessary to produce the vegetation density required to sustain humans based on their digestive capabilities. If the annual precipitation is less than this, the vegetation is too sparse and the humans have to cover an area that is too large in order to obtain enough food. To solve this dilemma, humans developed ways to utilize animals that had the abilities they lacked. The animals to be kept should be able to wander while grazing and be able to digest cellulose. In addition, these animals should possess a third important quality. In order to be able to utilize the milk, fat, or protein that the animals had produced from the digested biomass during the day, the humans had to ensure that the animals would come back to them regularly.

Thus, animal husbandry was discovered. This prevailed initially in the desert margins and is connected with nomadism. While grazing, the animals cover a radius of at least 10 to 20 km daily. They are able to harvest significantly more vegetation than humans could ever do and thus utilize a significantly larger amount of water in the arid areas. The animals are herded into protected, fenced-in areas at night and are milked or slaughtered as food for their herders. If in these regions the animals were to graze the same area on the following day, there would be too little grass for them to survive. Thus, in these unproductive regions, in order to cover their daily caloric requirements, the animals and their herders have to move on and continually find new grazing land. In these regions, human survival is based on utilizing animals which serve as "autonomous grazing machines" and calorie collectors, having a much larger operating radius than humans do. Through utilizing the animals, humans have a mechanism that daily harvests food over a large area. However, the growth of this grazed vegetation is based on a very low green water flow due to the sparse rain. By keeping these animals, humans are able to utilize this otherwise unusably low green water flow. But in this strategy, a large part of the calories in the grazed vegetation is needed by the animals themselves. Only a small part is stored as milk, fat, or protein by them and can be utilized by humans as food. Even though this strategy is very ineffective with respect to human utilization of the green water flow, because it uses the animals as an intermediate station, it is employed because it ensures the survival of a small population by utilizing large areas.

The nomadism in arid areas described above is long-established and in principle sustainable. However, in practice it leads to a slowly increasing population. This therefore leads to a slow increase in the number of animals that need to be kept to feed this population. At first, expanding the grazing area solves this problem. However, when the available grazing area is completely occupied, the only alternative is to increase the stock of animals, which results in over-grazing of the vegetation. Thus, the vegetation cannot recover and the consequence is a decline in the vegetation density. This then leads to a decline in the evaporation of water from the soil and to a reduction in precipitation. Thus, one is on the precipitous path of positive feedback between evaporation and precipitation, the end of which is a desert. This process is called desertification. This explains the expansion of the deserts at the expense of pastureland. According to the UN-Convention to Combat Desertification, two-thirds of the world's desert margins, and thus the pastureland in the arid areas, have been over-grazed and thus have not been used sustainably. This means that, worldwide, 50,000 km^2 of pastureland are lost to desert each year (SDNP, 2006).

At the other end of the precipitation scale, in the tropical rainforests, humans also started utilizing the environment very early. In contrast to the desert margins, water supply was never a problem, since dependable and sufficient precipitation falls in the humid tropics. The problem in these regions is the low soil fertility. Tropical soils are very old and have been subjected to the weathering process for millions of years. In this long period, the nutrients and minerals have been almost completely washed out by the precipitation. The vegetation survives in these regions first and foremost through their own decay as well as from dust that is blown into the tropical rainforests by atmospheric circulation. At first, humans were able to adapt to these conditions of nutrient limitation with their own sustainable strategy. Developing the ability to create fire deliberately was a great help here. By means of a deliberately-laid fire, the minerals and fertilizers contained in the vegetation could be set free at once and in high concentrations as ashes and thus be used for agriculture. This practice is called "slash and burn." The burned areas are at first very fertile because of the high mineral concentrations in the ashes and very good harvests are possible. The high temperatures and high amounts of precipitation are also helpful. However, the intensive storms in these regions wash away a large part of the ashes after only a few years. This reduces the fertility of the soil and agricultural production breaks down. The only strategy for survival for the population involved is to move on and slash and burn the next area of rainforest and repeat the process. The discarded, leached-out area can recover in about 40 to 100 years if it is not used. In principle, this type of utilization would be sustainable if there were no increase in population, which leads to a shortage of areas left to regenerate.

Thus, the only successful strategy here is also to move on. This strategy breaks down if the area available are not sufficient for the population increase. This is happening in all tropical rainforests, and thus today for the most part this way of life belongs to the past. The "modern" strategy is to burn down the rainforest and use artificial fertilizers and pesticides to stabilize the yield of the deforested areas.

Humans originated in the savannas of Africa. During our early development, we spent most of the time as nomads. This was possible because back then, the population density was low and thus at the dawn of mankind the available surface area was perceived as an infinite resource. The imprinting of this perception on early mankind has certainly not fostered the capability to think in terms of sustainability, resilience of the life-support system, or intergenerational justice.

5.5 People became farmers

In other regions, the nomadism described above did not become dominant. This is especially true for regions with sufficient precipitation, so that animals and humans had enough food without being forced to continually wander due to limited re-growth. In these cases, it is more advantageous for the humans to use the green water flow directly instead of leaving it mainly to animals. In place of the ineffective, indirect use by animals, humans chose to use the green water flow directly to produce crops in rain-fed agriculture.

Agricultural areas have therefore spread particularly in regions with sufficient precipitation and suitable soils. This is especially true for the eastern parts of China, for India, for East Africa, Europe, for an agricultural belt that stretches through Russia from west to east becoming narrower on the way, and, last but not least, in the last 300 years, for the eastern part and the prairies of the USA and Canada. In the last three centuries, these regions have undergone three developments, which have led to an expansion of the area under cultivation:

1   Massive clear-cutting of forests in all regions. This started in China, India, and Europe. In these regions, forests made up the natural vegetation.
2   Extensive draining of bogs and wetlands. In the temperate zone, extensive drainage programs, especially in the 19th century, led to an expansion of cropland at the expense of

natural areas. Drainage systems were installed in wetlands and bogs and thus these areas were "freed" of the excess water that made them unsuitable for agriculture.

3 Widespread expansion of farmland into the wet grasslands of the temperate zones, in particular in Russia and then also in North America.

Naturally, there are also large areas that were transformed from forest into pastures. These areas are located mainly in the tropical areas of Brazil, where parts of the deforested Amazon basin have been converted to cattle ranches, in order to satisfy the increasing international demand for meat.

In areas where the climate was too dry for agriculture, but where nevertheless sufficient water was available, sooner or later irrigation developed. The first large-scale irrigation cultivation cultures in Mesopotamia, China, and Egypt are examples of this. While both of the previously described strategies for nomadism were intelligent, but only marginally dependent upon the use of technical equipment, and while rain-fed agriculture only requires simple technical abilities, irrigation is connected with the development of comprehensive technological capabilities. This development began about 7000 years ago and first required the acquisition of the basic capability to transport water. The development of this capability was certainly not trivial. There was no understanding of the water cycle, nor of the role that slopes play, nor of the amounts of water. At first ditches were dug to redirect the water. To do this, primitive tools were developed. These first man-made technological activities were a breakthrough. They allowed the previously unimaginable redesigning of nature: making farmland out of desert. It is not astounding that this technological breakthrough occurred in the area of water management. Water was the limiting resource, which when mastered in the concerned regions, the arid areas, would result in the biggest effect concerning the production of food.

Thousands of years later, in a second revolutionary step, more high-tech developments occurred in irrigation technology. These were in particular: wells to provide water; pumps and other machinery to obtain water; gates to control the water flow; and masonry canals for leak-free transportation of the water. The second water revolution was much more far-reaching than the first. In particular, it became apparent that highly developed technical systems only brought about the desired success if they were complemented and supported by other cultural accomplishments. Thus, water rights came into being, which regulated the peaceful access of individual members of a society to the irrigation water. At first, the religions were responsible for the formulation and enforcement of water rights. The first regulations concerning water allocation dealt with the precise stipulations for the opening of the sluice-gates to water the fields. This method is still applied in many regions on Earth. Only the much later introduction of procedures able to measure the amounts of water allowed the determination of its specific allotment and thus the determination of prices for it.

The further steps that led to the large-scale technical hydraulic projects, such as at the Aral Sea or the Nile, appear to be only a consequential further development, as compared to the second water revolution, and not as another revolution in themselves. In both regions, large new agricultural areas were created through the utilization of irrigation. The use of irrigation water increased the flow of green water at the expense of that of blue water. This can, as in the case of the Colorado River in the western USA or the Yellow River in China, lead to former mighty rivers no longer reaching the ocean, since all of the water is used for transpiration. The consequences for navigation, power generation, and above all for the aquatic communities in the rivers are drastic.

If the man-made impacts described are connected with the values for the transpiration coefficients for the selected crops that are listed in Table 4, it becomes abundantly clear how land use changes affect water flow.

Assuming constant precipitation, loss of forests is generally accompanied by a loss of assimilated carbon and thus dry biomass. However, since forests generally evaporate more than grasslands or cultivated fields, an increase in the blue water flow due to clear-cutting is to be expected. The conversion of forests into pasture and farmland resulted in an increase in the risks of flooding due to increased discharge as well as an increase in the risk of droughts due to the reduced water storage capabilities of agricultural areas as compared to forests.

The intensive use of the arid areas of the planet for large cattle stocks decreases the productivity of these regions due to the reduction of the vegetation cover. This also reduces transpiration and thus the green water flow. This can then lead to the feedback process described above, which then eventually leads to desertification.

The rain-fed agriculture in our temperate zone also leads to a change in the water balance. If the areas are too wet for cultivation, they have to be drained. Plants that are grown instead of the original ones need more water to build dry mass. Finally, introducing irrigation is the most direct way to change the water balance through land use. This redirects the blue water flow directly into green water flow. Thus, the formidable restructuring of nature that humans have carried out to ensure their food supply has also brought about a corresponding change in the blue and green water flow.

5.6 People are city dwellers

Along with the explosive population growth of the last decades, man-made changes in land use have entered a new phase: global urbanization. This is not yet visible in Fig. 20, since its percentage of the total area is still too low. However, this will change in the next twenty-five years. Around 1900, only 5% of Africa's population lived in cities, today it is more than 40%, and in twenty years it will be 70%. Thus, urbanization will be much faster than the global expansion of agricultural and animal husbandry in the past 300 years.

People organize themselves in communities. Even in areas with very low population densities, humans are not loners, but prefer to form tribes and villages. The human instinct to form social communities has led to larger and larger settlements. Tribes become villages, villages become cities, and more recently, cities become mega-cities, settlements with populations of more than ten million people. The largest human settlement, Greater Tokyo, now houses thirty-five million people and no end to the global aggregation of settlements is in sight. The year that this book was first published will become a noted date in the history of urbanization: in 2007, for the first time, there were more people living in cities than in the country. And all predictions confirm that the tendency towards urbanization will continue. Accordingly, 70% of the population will live in cities in 2025. And the urbanization process is a long way from being finished.

The trend towards urbanization in Europe, which is more or less finished, and where more than 75% of the population lives in cities, is connected with drastic changes in lifestyle. This trend was accompanied by the industrialization and the change from the rural lifestyle of the 18th century to the industrial lifestyles of the 19th and early 20th centuries. Peasants and agricultural laborers went to the cities to find a better future for their children. By being able to burn fossil fuels, factories employed powered machinery and rationalized their production processes. Markets expanded thanks to the increased buying power of broad levels of the population. In the development of the cities, it became apparent that due to the increased density of the population, certain important markets, such as the employment market, consumer goods market and services such health and educa-tion, could be organized with far greater efficiency than in rural areas. There, the long transport distances and the small selec-tion of goods and services due to the low population density led to goods being more expensive. After all, the development of the individual transport paradoxically originated in the cities through the development of cars. Actually, owing to the long dis-tances there, individual transport should have been more impor-tant in rural areas, but there it was unaffordable.

In the meantime, all of the cities in the developing countries are experiencing massive growth due to the influx of people. In doing so, similar developments as in Europe in the 19th and the early 20th century take place. For example, the population of Dar es Salaam, the former capital of Tanzania, doubles every 13 years. This means that it increases three times faster than the population of the country, which increases only 2% per year. The growth process is similar in all cities of the Third World and is driven by people's dreams of escaping rural poverty by moving to the more prosperous city centers. In between is the pitiless poverty belt of the slums, which must be conquered if one wants to acquire education and prosperity for one's children. With the present annual economic growth rates of 6–10% in many regions of the world, millions of jobs are being generated in the cities of the emerging economies of China, India, Brazil, and South Africa. These jobs nourish the dream of prosperity, which is the motor of urbanization processes and of the growth of the cities.

In the meantime in many places, the growth of the cities has switched over to a paradoxical phase. Cities are undermining their own existence by their growth and by the expansion of urban lifestyles. Their survival is dependent upon a constant influx of goods and services from the surrounding area. This influx is not just people, but above all also food, water, and energy. However, their expansion devours the agricultural land in the surrounding areas upon which their survival is based. In addition, unfortunately this process is often destroying very fertile agricultural land, because these expanding cities were founded in regions that had very fertile surroundings. Thus a disastrous process starts, which ends with the conversion of large areas of agricultural land into tenement blocks, factories, airports, streets, parking lots, golf courses, and tennis courts.

If we assume that for every million people that are born now 40,000 hectares of land are needed for cities (Brown, 2004), this means that the seventy million people that are born every year require three million hectares of new land annually. Generally, these are fertile agricultural areas, since they are near cities. During the next twenty years, this inescapable development will destroy sixty million hectares of agricultural land worldwide, an area equal to the entire cultivable area of Europe. This is alarming and certainly not sustainable.

Whereas the population growth accelerates the building of houses and factories, economic growth inevitably increases the number of cars, especially in China, India, Brazil, and southern Africa. Cars need room, just as their owners do. Presently, the number of cars worldwide is increasing by nine million annually. In addition to every car, the area needed to drive it on as well as to park it also increases. The area assigned to cars varies worldwide and ranges between 0.07 hectares per car in sparsely populated countries such as the USA, Canada, or Brazil to 0.02 hectares per car in Europe, China, Japan, and India. For every million new cars, which the increasing prosperity in, for example, India generates, some 20,000 hectares of land must be converted to street and parking lots. Due to the sealing of the surfaces, these areas lose the capability to evaporate water. Thus, the million cars destroy the green water flow of the areas they take over. In India this is estimated to be about seventy-five million m^3 annually. This amount of water could be used to grow 50,000 tons of grain in India, enough to feed 250,000 people (Brown, 2004). The conversion and the corresponding sealing of the surfaces means that at the first point of division in Fig. 17, the precipitation has no access to any path except surface discharge. This is noticeable in particular during heavy precipitation events, where direct surface runoff leads to a strong increase in flooding, analogous to the case of clear-cutting shown in Fig. 18. Floods lead to the fastest possible transport of precipitation away from the land to the ocean, since the vast amounts of water that were once stored by nature cannot be sufficiently stored in dams. However, this run-off cannot be further utilized.

Urbanization is proceeding dynamically and is accompanied in the countries involved by great expectations and dreams of prosperity and consumption. For example, China is planning to convert the fertile 100-km corridor between its capital, Beijing, and the city of Tianjin on the coast, both already megacities, into a large common urban entity within the next twenty years. That means that the cultivable land between both cites will be covered with houses, factories, streets, parking lots, shopping centers, and hopefully also golf courses. After all, 100 million people are supposed to live and work in this emerging megacity. Whether such mammoth entities are even viable, how large their surroundings can and must be, what the blue and green water flow that is required to provide such megacities with vital goods will be like, how the transport systems will be set up, and what acceptable lives in such megacities might be like, and even more importantly, how this all is supposed to happen sustainably, all these questions are the most fascinating topics in current research.

5.7   People behave differently from the Earth system

A strategy can be identified in our utilization of the Earth's natural resources up to now, and this includes the green water flow. This strategy consists of population growth and providing vital goods such as food and housing through targeted changes to the Earth's surface. To achieve this, there is only one possibility: changing the vegetation cover and thus land use. The use of green water for food production is determined by the agricultural practices employed. Fields are used to grow crops. Agriculture also has a second strategy in store for further optimization of the land use, by providing for an increase in plant growth and thus for an increase in productivity of the ecosystems concerned.

In general, natural ecosystems suffer from nutrient limitation. Through the addition of nitrogen and phosphate fertilizers as well as any minerals that are lacking, the amount of biomass grown per unit area can be significantly increased. However, this also means that the amount of water that evaporates increases. Since the development of technologies to manufacture nitrogen fertilizer from atmospheric nitrogen by Haber and Bosch at the start of the last century, the natural nutrient limitation on crops has been practically abolished throughout large parts of the world. Fig. 21 shows a comparison of the amount of worldwide

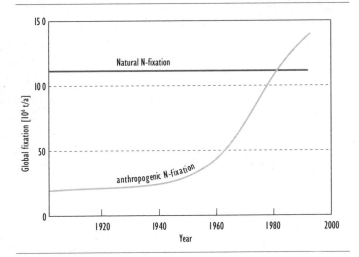

Figure 21   Comparison of the temporal development of the natural and
man-made nitrogen fixation as the conversion of atmospheric
nitrogen (N_2) into biologically useable nitrogen (NO_x and
NH_x) (from Geographie, 2007, after Vitousek, 1994)

nitrogen fixation with the amount that was industrially produced
and used in agriculture to increase the yield.

According to present knowledge, natural nitrogen fixation has
hardly changed in the course of the last century. Worldwide, it is
about 110 million tons of nitrogen per year. Among the natural
processes of nitrogen fixation are symbioses between natural
vegetation and soil bacteria (rhizobium) as well as lightning
during storms. This is depicted as a horizontal line in Fig. 21.
The production of nitrogen fertilizer increased so much between
1960 and 1980 that it surpassed natural fixation in 1980. Examples of man-made nitrogen fixation are the transformation of
atmospheric nitrogen during the burning of hydrocarbons (e. g.

in cars), the industrial production of artificial fertilizers, and the agrarian use of rice, soy beans, and alfalfa, which convert atmospheric N_2 into nitrogen that can be biologically used by plants through symbiosis with soil bacteria.

The intersection of both curves in Fig. 21 depicts the point in time at which man-made nitrogen surpassed the amount of nitrogen produced by the Earth system. This date is memorable. It happened in approximately 1981 and is not mentioned in any history books. Nevertheless, for the first time in history, by using technology we succeeded in dominating an important and quantitatively large cycle of matter in the Earth system, namely the nitrogen cycle, and this not just in individual areas, but worldwide. Thus, 1981, a time when the word "globalization" had not yet taken on any real importance, marks the final globalization of man-made impact upon the Earth system.

The flattening of the rise in artificial nitrogen fixation since about 1980, as indicated in Fig. 21, continues. Now, nitrogen consumption is increasing globally only very slowly. This shows that in only sixty years, it was possible to abolish the natural nutrient deficit in agricultural areas on Earth.

This was linked to a deliberate and impressive rise in agricultural yields. The massive use of artificial fertilizers, together with the selection of new, high-yielding crops, was the prerequisite for the green revolution. It was needed to feed the increasing population and it freed countries such as India and China from hunger, where at this time more than one-third of the world's population lived. The rise in yield is clearly seen in Fig. 22.

Yet, why is the rise in agricultural productivity and thus the accompanying human dominance of the Earth's nitrogen cycle important for the green water flow? Eliminating the nutrient deficit from the cultivated fields results in increased productivity, which, because of the tight coupling of yield and water

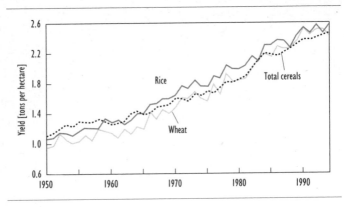

Figure 22 Yield increase of rice, wheat and cereals between 1950 and
1995 (from WBGU, 1997)

consumption via the transpiration coefficient (see Table 4), also
results in an increase in the area's water consumption.

5.8 Water for people and nature

Thus, looking at the rapid changes in land use and productivity
increases in the last decades, the answer to the question as to
whether humans have changed the green water flow is yes. Since
green water, as explained earlier, cannot have multiple uses, this
has far-reaching consequences for the water cycle and for the
water reserves available to the increasing world population in
the next generations and thus upon the issue that is the basis of
this book. We are approaching the crucial question: How much
can we increase the global green water flow to food production
without damaging the life-support system?

Humans have thoroughly changed the green water flow already.

Ecozone	Subzone	Rain (mm/a)	Blue water flow		Green water flow	
			Surface (mm/a)	Groundwater (mm/a)	Evaporation (mm/a)	Biomass (t/ha)
Subtropic and tropic	Desert savanna	300	18	2	280	2–6
	Dry savanna	1000	100	30	870	4–12
	Wet savanna	1850	360	240	1200	8–20
Subarctic – temperate	Tundra	370	70	40	260	1–2
	Taiga	700	160	140	400	10–15
	Mixed forest	750	150	100	500	10–15
	Forest steppe	650	90	30	530	8–12
Equatorial	Humid inner tropics	2000	600	600	800	30–50

Table 5 Division of the precipitation in blue and green water flow in different climate zones on Earth (after Falkenmark, 2004).

Has it also been increased? With the state of today's knowledge, this question cannot be answered precisely. As described earlier, not all human activities which lead to land-use changes, also lead to an increase in the green water flow. The obvious increase in the green water flow due to intensified agriculture and expansion of irrigation is opposed by a reduction due to draining of the wetlands and bogs as a result of soil amelioration measures, the reduction of the evaporation due to over-grazing of arid areas and the expansion of the deserts, as well as urbanization. Thus, the division of precipitation into blue and green water varies greatly between regions. Table 5 lists the best available figures on the division of precipitation for typical regions on Earth together with their respective production of biomass in tons per hectare.

Table 5 shows the large regional differences with regards to the division of precipitation into blue and green water. In the desert savannas, the blue water flow ceases almost entirely; most of the precipitation evaporates. With increasing water supply in the wet savanna, evaporation in this tropical region increases and reaches levels of up to 1200 mm/a, while generating between 8 and 20 tons of biomass per hectare. These values are not reached in the temperate zone, which includes Central Europe. In our latitudes, the evaporation of a mixed forest is about 500 mm/a, while producing 10 to 15 tons of biomass. The absolute front-runners in biomass production are the tropical rainforests. Here an evaporation of 800 mm/a can achieve a biomass production of 30 to 50 tons per hectare. That is also where the blue water flow is the greatest, which is very impressively confirmed by the immense water flows of the Amazon and Congo Rivers. Overall, regional differences in the division of precipitation into blue and green water flow are large. The largest flow of blue water on Earth exists in the tropical rainforests and wet savannas. This is due to the high levels of precipitation and the limited levels of evaporation.

The values in Table 5 can be extrapolated to determine the amount of water used by people and how much water is left to nature. To do this, the percentage of the area covered by the respective ecozones and subzones must be known. Finally, the respective water flow must be considered in terms of its primary control by humans or by the Earth's life-support system to ensure its integrity. For example, the green water flow in all of the steppes and grasslands on Earth is now significantly controlled by humans. People decide upon the number of animals that graze the area and thus for the most part, the density of the vegetation. Naturally this is also the case on an even larger scale for pastures. Table 6 shows a global overview of the size of the blue and green water flow.

The amount of precipitation amount on the continents forms the total water resources shown in Table 6. This amount is equal

Water flow	Eco-/Use System	Water consumption [km2/a]	Percentage of precipitation [%]
Blue for humans	Irrigation	2100	2
	Households/Industry	1300	1
Blue for nature	River ecology through base flow	9400	8
	Flood flow	30,150	27
Sub-total blue		42,650	38
Green for humans	Dry farming	5000	4
	Pasture farming	20,400	18
	Steppe/Grasslands	12,100	11
Green for nature	Forest and shrubbery	19,700	17
	Deserts	5700	5
	Wetlands	1400	1
	Lake evaporation	760	1.1
	Evaporation Parks	100	0.1
	Rest	5390	4.8
Sub-total green		70,850	62
Total		113,500	100

Table 6 Global overview of the blue and green water flow in km3/a (after Falkenmark, 2004)

to the sum of blue and green water flows. Both large categories, the blue and green water flow, are shown in different background shades. The total water flow is shown in gray. With these two categories the respective flows are distinguished according to their main use by humans for survival or by nature to maintain the integrity of the life-support system. The second column in

Table 6 shows the pathways by which precipitation is distributed on Earth.

Annually, a total amount of 113,500 km³ of precipitation falls on the Earth's surface. This is 100% of the available fresh water. Almost 40% of the precipitation, 42,650 km³, becomes blue water. Only a small part, 3400 km³, is used by humans for irrigation and to meet domestic or industrial demands. The amount of precipitation that is used for irrigation is converted to green water and removed as water vapor by the wind.

At first glance, the degree of utilization of blue water by people, less than 10%, seems surprisingly small. However, only the extraction of blue water from the rivers and lakes is taken into account here. The wide range of impacts to water resources through its use, i.e. storage in dams, decrease in water quality through pollution, the use of blue water for cooling and energy production, was not considered in Table 6. If more than just this withdrawal of water is considered, such as the more far-reaching human control of the water in the lakes and rivers, a totally different picture for the blue water flow arises.

For similar reasons, which were also decisive for the construction of the Aswan High Dam, the 20th century was characterized by the construction of water retention structures such as dams and impounding dams throughout the world. Their task is to regulate the blue water flow. Fig. 23 shows the increase in water volume that is regulated by large dams worldwide. The extent to which the regulation of the blue water flow by dams has increased, particularly between 1960 and 1990, is easily discernable. A discharge with the total volume of ca. 15,000 km³/a is currently regulated by dams. According to Table 6, this is almost 40% of the annual discharge in rivers worldwide.

In spite of the dams, the major part of blue water can be used as base flow or in floods by nature to maintain life in the

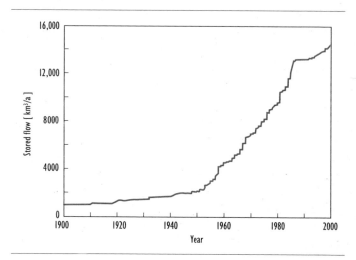

Figure 23 Development of the water flow controlled by the large dams
on Earth in km³/a (after Alcamo et al., 2005)

lakes and rivers. The aquatic life in rivers is dependent upon a
minimal flow for survival, especially in times of low precipitation. If this is not maintained, the aquatic communities in the
rivers and lakes are damaged and in the end, so is the capability
of these bodies to purify the water and remove contaminants.
Water purification is an essential service provided by the rivers
and lakes. Principally, animals and plants in the rivers and lakes
require this service in order to maintain livable habitats. However,
humans also increasingly use it to remove our civilization's waste
products and surplus fertilizer. If the natural aquatic ecosystems
should lose the capability to carry out this service, theoretically
humans would have to replace it by investing in new, much more
complex sewage treatment plants. Today's sewage treatment
plants operate comparatively economically by removing only the

worst waste products and leaving the remaining complex purification processes to nature. The crux of the matter is that these new sewage treatment plants would have to be as complex as the destroyed aquatic ecosystem, in order to provide the same services. Besides the fact that such complex treatment plants do not yet exist (and most likely never will), their cost would be exorbitant and would most likely far exceed the seeming benefits which began the process of destroying these aquatic ecosystems.

The second section of Table 6 shows the green water flow, displayed here with a white background. This flow is also subdivided into green flow that is regulated by humans and green flow that is currently used almost entirely by nature to maintain the integrity and stability of the Earth's life support system. With over 70,000 km^3/a, the green water flow is much larger than the blue water flow. Today, the green water that is used to grow crops amounts to 5000 km^3/a and is more than twice as much as the total irrigation water used worldwide. Nevertheless, the permanent pasture farming in the transformed prairies of North and South America, in the savannas of Africa, and in the steppes of Asia requires 20,400 km^3/a, which is four times as much green water for meat production as actual agriculture today. In addition to this there is the often still nomadic, yet almost always over-grazed use of the sparse vegetation in the arid areas of the desert margins, with another 12,100 km^3 of green water per year. All together, humans now regulate a gigantic green water flow of 37,500 km^3/a. This green water flow is almost completely used to maintain the food supply.

The green water flow that is hardly regulated by humans and thus is almost completely available for the natural stabilization of the Earth system is essentially used for transpiration from forests and scrublands, wetlands, rivers, and lakes. In addition to this, there is also a small amount of evaporation from the ice sheets and deserts. This amount, 27,660 km^3/a, seems very large. Transpiration in the forests and scrublands occurs exclusively under biological control. In these areas, the biosphere can fulfill its global task to regulate the concentration of the greenhouse gases, water vapor and CO_2, and thus the temperature, as well as to maximize biodiversity to ensure the stability of the biosphere.

The services that the Earth system provides with the blue water flow, during the self-purification of rivers etc., are regional by nature. They pertain to a section of river, a lake, or an area of wetland. This is different to the services provided by the green water flow. Here, important global tasks are also accomplished. In addition to food production, which is actually a regional task, the green water flow also contributes to balancing of greenhouse gases and thus regulating the Earth's temperature and producing oxygen. These global services of the green water flow differ in two important aspects from the regional services of the blue water flow. On the one hand, every local impact upon the green water flow affects the global services of the Earth system and thus automatically has an impact upon the entire planet. For example, the impact upon the Earth's thermostat due to logging operations in the rainforests and their conversion to fields and pastures in Brazil affects not only those people living on that river, but all humans and ecosystems on Earth. On the other hand, not all global services can be equally replaced or supported by technology, as evidenced by the natural self-purification of aquatic ecosystems compared to the performance of a sewage treatment plant. A technological substitute for the development of biodiversity in natural ecosystems is unimaginable. It is not even known which species would be the best to "create" artificially. A globally-effective oxygen production device, which would replace the oxygen that is lost by converting natural ecosystems to agricultural production has not yet been discovered, nor is it envisaged. As it is, we will most likely determine that the most cost-effective and optimized device for this purpose is the one we are in the process of destroying, namely undisturbed nature.

5.9 Summary

Before humans began to utilize the Earth's water resources for their own purposes, 100% of them were utilized by nature. Even then, the precipitation was probably divided into approximately 60% green and 40% blue water flow. Both types of flow were exclusively used to stabilize Earth's life-support system and performed important services, such as the regulation of greenhouse gases and thus the stabilization of the planet's temperature, the purification and processing of plant and animal waste products, and the storage of water in the soil. Since then, humans have become the main agents in dividing the water flow on Earth. They considerably expanded the area of agricultural fields and pastures in the last 300 years, but even more so in more recent decades. Thus, the green water flow that essentially flowed through forests and wetlands has now been redirected through crops and pastures. These plants deal with water much less effectively than forests. However, they directly or indirectly produce useful food. In addition, the expansion of irrigation with its connected redirection of parts of the blue and green water flow occurred. Even if humans have only increased the green water flow slightly, in the past thirty to forty years, they have acquired worldwide control over a large part of the green water flow. The green water that is regulated by the humans comprises some 60% of the total green water flow on the planet. The remaining part is not regulated by the farmers with their livestock, but rather by nature itself. If fertilizers are not used to increase plant growth, it

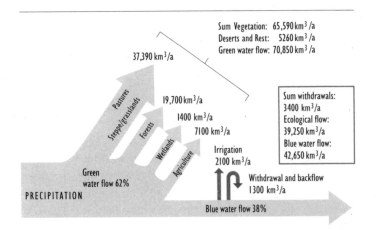

Figure 24 Green and blue water flow in regions with tropical and temperate climates (after Falkenmark, 2001)

is regulated through the natural supply of nutrients. Likewise, if pesticides are not used to protect the vegetation, vegetation and pests are ensnared in continuous, selective competition. The rules governing how green water is used by humans and by nature are obviously very different.

Fig. 24 shows a summary of the global division of precipitation into blue and green water flow. The conclusion is that in the course of the changes in the last 300 years and in particular the second half of the last century, humans have acquired control over the water flow on the continents of Earth. They not only regulate the division of the precipitation at the relevant points on the surface and in the soil differently from the way nature does, they have also learned to store water and to utilize it at times that nature never would have, as the example of the Nile demonstrated.

6 How Much Water Do People Need?

In the last chapter, I dealt with the water consumption by humans and nature quantitatively. The result was that already today, approximately 60% of the green and 40% of the blue water flow on the surface of the Earth is regulated by humans. This is a formidable accomplishment and quite a lot of thought and effort was required to achieve this.

Why did we humans expend this thought and effort converting large parts of the Earth's surface and redirecting mighty water flows? What do we do with so much water?

Water is used in three core areas:

- as drinking water and for sanitation purposes
- in industries
- for food production (transpiration water).

Both of the first two uses are direct uses of blue water, the third is indirect use of green water.

While I was writing this book, there were 6.5 billion people living on this planet (U. S. Census Bureau, 2006). In the next few years, an estimated 78 million people will be added each year. This corresponds to almost the entire population of Germany. Our survival, but especially that of the people in arid regions, depends upon changes in the Earth's water cycle. If we want to reconcile water used by nature and water used by humans, it is important to understand the minimum amount of water that people require to ensure their basic needs.

6.1 Drinking water

In order to survive, everyone needs 3–5 liters of drinking water per day. On a global scale, this is not much. The entire amount of drinking water that the world population would need for a year is about 10 km^3. It would fit in a cube with 2.1 km edges. This amount corresponds to barely ten-thousandths of the worldwide amount of precipitation or four-thousandths of the blue water flow on Earth. Thus, there is no danger of running out of drinking water in the foreseeable future, especially since, to a certain extent, it can be used multiple times. However, the high quality requirements of drinking water are a problem in many areas. Contamination of the blue water flow through other uses, e.g. industrial or agricultural fertilizers and pesticides, correspondingly reduces drinking water resources and either raises its processing costs or leads to health problems such as those described in the Aral Sea.

6.2 Sanitary water

Healthy living conditions presume proper hygiene, clean food and clothes, the removal of waste and its subsequent, preferably comprehensive, decomposition and conversion to nutrients. These were the prerequisites for eradicating the serious cholera, typhus, and other epidemics that afflicted Europe in the Middle Ages and early modern times and cost millions of lives. Even back then, in order to provide the increasing population with proper hygiene and to ensure removal and decomposition of waste, the natural transport paths via streams and streets, as well as the washing-out of feces through precipitation, were no longer sufficient. Nowadays, no one doubts that hygienic conditions in villages and cities, especially with increased population densities, are best achieved by water supply networks, canalization systems, and sewage treatment plants. These need a minimum water flow to function, which is estimated to be between 20 and 40 liters per person per day and thus five to ten times more than requirement for drinking water.

Thus, water consumption of between 20 and 40 liters per person per day is the minimum amount that a person needs to lead a healthy, decent life (Falkenmark, 2004). To do this, 1.5 to 3 per mill of water would have to be taken out of the rivers worldwide. A large part would flow back into the rivers after being used and suitably cleaned. Even if much less water were available in a region, the question as to when humans will run out of water appears to be answered. The supply of drinking water and water needed for basic sanitation for the current 6.5 billion people on Earth is easily provided by the planet. Even if the number of people were to double in the next century, they could not use even a percentage of the available blue water flow. Thus, in terms of the amount of available blue water, drinking water and basic hygiene are ensured for the foreseeable future. At first, this appears to be a very reassuring perspective.

However, as is so often the case, reality does not care much about global considerations, but rather has regional concerns; people are affected regionally. Correspondingly, reality departs quite considerably from the reassuring picture that I have just painted. Approximately 2.6 billion people did not have access to basic hygiene facilities in 2004 and thus did not have access to the minimum amount of water needed for a healthy life (WHO/

UNICEF, 2004). Part of basic sanitary facilities is being connected to sewage system, being connected to a clean drinking water system, and having a flushing toilet or at least a sump. From a Central European point of view, this is not asking very much. Two billion people, or 75% of the people, who do not have access to these basic facilities live in Asia, 18% in Africa, and 5% in Latin America and the Caribbean.

This cannot be because water is unavailable. There is enough drinking and sanitation water available even in very dry regions. What are lacking are the facilities and municipal infrastructures that could operate these systems in a sustainable way.

Much has been done in this area in the last few decades, but not yet enough. Between 1990 and 2000, an estimated one billion people were provided with the services described. Thus, international efforts to improve the living conditions on Earth have been immensely successful. However, this success has been overwhelmed by the explosion of population growth. Even after a decade of extreme effort, the unfortunate result was that, when seen as a whole, instead of a billion more people having access to clean water, 500 million more people had no access in 2000 as compared to 1990. Like Sisyphus, we are fighting here against a rapidly increasing world population. We have achieved so much in the last decade, but have hardly improved anything. As a result, in southern Africa, the population suffering bad sanitary conditions has even risen from 32% in 1990 to 36% in 2002. On the other hand, the formerly high numbers in Oceania dropped sharply between 1990 and 2000. In addition, East Asia has also reported large advances (SIWI, 2004).

Falling below the minimum blue water flow of 20 to 40 liters per day and thus suffering the consequent bad hygienic conditions has dramatic consequences. The lack of access to clean water, sanitary facilities, and a minimum standard of basic hygiene are the main causes of waterborne illnesses. These include first and foremost the bacterial diarrhetic illnesses such as cholera, typhoid, and dysentery and viral illnesses such as polio and hepatitis A, but also a wide range of parasitic diseases. Waterborne diseases pose the third largest health risk in the developing world. In addition, even the largest health risk worldwide, being underweight due to malnutrition, is often caused by bad water and poor hygiene. The most frequent consequences of bad drinking and sanitation water are diarrhetic diseases. Many mothers, who suffer from malnutrition, are so weakened by diarrhetic diseases that they cannot feed their children. Many children die of starvation because they cannot retain nourishment due to this diarrhea. Approximately 2.3 million deaths per year are the result of three closely related factors: no clean water, no sanitary facilities, and no basic standards of hygiene. It is especially tragic that 90% of the deaths are children under five years of age.

A recent study, carried out by Fewtrell (2005), clearly showed the effects of introducing clean water, sanitary facilities, and basic hygiene. He investigated to what degree different measures would reduce death rates due to diarrhetic diseases. These were his results:

- An improvement in the water supply would reduce the death rate due to diarrhetic diseases by 6% to 25%. This is especially so for the most dangerous diseases such as cholera and typhoid.
- An improvement in sanitary facilities would reduce the death rate due to diarrhetic diseases on average by 32%.
- An improvement in hygienic conditions together with improved education and promoting the washing of hands would reduce the death rate on average by 45%.
- An improvement in the quality of the drinking water

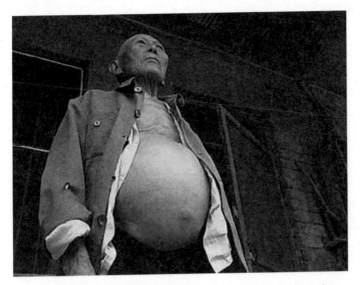

Figure 25   A fisherman infected with schistosomiasis in Jiangxi province
in China (W. B. Zouh)

through measures undertaken by the end user such as
on-site chlorination, boiling, and clean storage can lead to
an additional reduction in the death rate due to diarrhetic
diseases by 35%.

These figures clearly show how directly water quality, sanitary
facilities, and basic hygiene can have a positive effect upon one's
health. The positive influence of improved sanitary conditions
goes far beyond diarrhetic diseases. There are six further disease
patterns in which a positive effect upon the health of the population due to improved water supply, sanitary facilities, and basic
hygiene could be proven.

Seen globally, these diseases are important as well. It is

estimated that 160 million people are infected with schistosomes. Schistosomiasis (also known as bilharzia, bilharziosis or snail fever) is a parasitic disease that is caused by several species of fluke (flatworms) and mainly infects fishermen and rice farmers. It leads to painful infestation of the internal organs, as can be seen in Fig. 25. An estimated 133 million people suffer from parasitic infestation of round-, whip-, and hook-worms and there are frequently drastic consequences such as serious dysentery, anemia, or pneumonia.

Disease	Number of dead children under 4 years of age [millions]	Total deaths [millions]
Respiratory diseases	2.4	4.35
Diarrhetic diseases	2.1	2.3
Malaria	1.6	1.7
HIV/AIDS	0.45	3.3
Tuberculosis	0	2.1

Table 7 Cause of death for children under four years of age and the total number of deaths in developing countries 2002 (SIWI, 2004)

Worldwide, waterborne diseases are among the greatest threats to humans. From a global viewpoint, according to Table 7, more people die from diarrhetic diseases than from tuberculosis or malaria. And tragically, most of the dead are children. Diarrhetic diseases often occur in combination with other diseases and weaken the patients even more. In addition, poor hygiene often affects the care given by relatives to the patient.

By far the worst damage caused by waterborne diseases have to do with the millions of people who are afflicted. Diarrhea caused by polluted water, and the accompanying weakening of the afflicted person, increases poverty. It ties up the workforce, in particular women, who have to nurse their sick relatives. In addition, the women are forced to undertake daily marches to find water and carry it back over long distances. Also, constant diarrhea hinders the children's education and reduces their chances for a successful future. Thus in many places, diarrhetic diseases are often the start of an almost hopeless vicious circle that begins with inadequate basic hygiene, resulting in unproductive work by the parents, which leads to early death due to illness, which is followed by illness and inadequate education for the children. When these children grow older and start a family, poverty is predetermined and inadequate hygiene results once again.

Thus, there is a momentous dimension hidden behind the succinct statement that we only need between 20 and 40 liters of water a day. The question as to how long our water resources will last is, in terms of our supplies of drinking water and water for adequate sanitation, firstly a question of water quality and only then a question of the amount of water. Several billion people suffer worldwide because of poor-quality water. Thus, the fear that they might die of thirst in the future is hardly important if they die before this due to water-borne diseases.

6.3 Water for industry

The manufacture of industrial products is dependent upon water in many ways. Water is used to generate the energy that is used to refine agricultural products, e.g. by brewing beer. It is used to cool industrial processes, such as in generating energy or in making steel. Water also cleans goods, e.g. in the semi-conductor industries, as well as removing industrial waste.

Industries use blue water almost exclusively. The main

Year	Paper industry	Chemical industry	Oil and coal industries	Heavy industry	Processing industry
1954	2.4	1.6	3.3	1.3	1.8
1959	3.1	1.6	4.4	1.5	2.2
1964	2.7	2.0	4.4	1.5	2.1
1968	2.9	2.1	5.1	1.6	2.3
1973	3.4	2.7	6.4	1.8	2.9
1978	5.3	2.9	7.0	1.9	3.4
1985	6.6	13.2	18.3	6.0	8.6
2000	11.8	28.0	32.7	12.3	17.1

Table 8 The rate of re-use of water as number of re-uses of a specific volume of water in various sectors of German industry (after WBGU, 1997)

industrial uses of water are cooling thermal power plants, generating energy, paper and cellulose production, cement production, and refining crude oil. During these industrial processes, only a small part of the water is used up. Primarily, the composition and properties of the water are changed. These changes range from harmless ones such as heating and household waste disposal, to the accumulation of acids and toxic substances in sewage from factories. In this case, the relationship between upstream and downstream riparian sites is very important. In particular, through its use or respectively its contamination, an upstream riparian site can render the water unfit for further use downstream. Industrial processes are especially suited for multiple usages of the same water if the upstream and downstream users belong to the same company. In these cases, as already happens in many companies, the cost-effectiveness can be derived from a comprehensive cost-benefit analysis of the contamination and cleaning costs for the water. The degree of multiple uses of the water, i.e. the number of re-uses of a specific volume of water, is highly dependent upon the sector and the technologies used. In extreme cases, such as the Audi factory in Ingolstadt, over 98% of the water used in car production is re-used.

Table 8 shows the historical development of the rate of re-use of water for various industries in Germany. The rate of re-use is thus about three times as high in the oil and coal industries as in heavy industries. Table 8 also impressively shows how much the rate of re-use has increased in the past few decades in Germany. This is particularly due to the increased utilization of waste heat recovery from water used for cooling. After removing the heat from the water that was used in the cooling process, the water can be re-used for cooling without any problems.

An examination of the use of water in industrial processes shows that a cost-benefit analysis carried out throughout the entire process with simultaneous development of suitable technologies to treat the water would lead to a massive increase in the rate of re-use. This provides a first indication as to the extent the rate of re-use of river water worldwide could be increased, if comprehensive management of water resources, including upstream and downstream riparian interests, would take place.

Naturally, it is difficult to determine industrial water consumption quantitatively due to the numerous industries as well as the varying degree of contamination of the water through different industrial processes. The values range from less than 10 m³ per person per year for developing countries and up to 140 m³ per person per year for industrialized countries. The industrial water consumption of the highly developed countries in Western Europe is now decreasing, primarily due to the increased re-use of water. Another large reduction in Western European industrial water use is due to the fact that water-intensive industries have now relocated some of their production to emerging economies

Direct water consumption [m3 per person per year]			
	USA	Europe	Africa
Households	100	57	10
Services	140	35	8
Industries	126	140	7
Sum	366	232	25

Table 9 Direct water consumption according to regions and sectors
       (after Falkenmark, 2004)

such as China, India, Brazil, and South Africa. The most reliable figure for the average industrial water consumption is the value of 130 liters per person per day, which is based on the thorough analyses by Shiklomanov (2000).

In this section, we have tried to look at how much water humans need for a decent, healthy life and came up with the amount of 20 to 40 liters per day. On average, this corresponds to a total of about 11 m³ water per year. What does our actual direct water consumption in the different regions of the planet look like? This is shown in Table 9.

These values show the great gap in the industrialized countries between the minimum amount needed and the actual amount used in households. In Africa, the average household water consumption is 10 m³ per person per year, which is almost exactly the minimal amount needed, 11 m³ per person per year. This means in practice that every second African uses too little water and every second African may use more than the minimum amount. In Europe, the household use is five times as high as the minimum and in the USA, it is ten times as high. In all three regions, there is enough water available for use. The only difference is the degree of development in the different parts of the world.

In summary, these observations are clear:

1 To a considerable degree, our health is determined by securing hygienic conditions through the availability of sufficient water for drinking and sanitation.

2 Earth's life-support system can easily provide the amount of drinking and sanitation water that people need for a decent life. At this time, we use far less than 1 per cent of the blue water that is available worldwide. Thus, there is by far enough water available to ensure an adequate drinking and sanitation water supply for all people. This also includes all those still to be born according to the usual prognoses on world population.

3 Even in regions with low precipitation, there is no lack of water for drinking and sanitation. If there are problems, it is because of inadequate distribution systems and bad management.

4 The further development of 2.6 billion people on Earth depends upon whether or not they receive access to clean drinking water, sanitary facilities, and improved basic hygiene. This is not a question of too little water, but rather a question of too little of money as well as too little political responsibility.

6.4 Water for food

Although the crucial question of this book, "How long will our water resources last" has been answered surprisingly clearly and positively as regards water for drinking and sanitation, it is not so clear or simple with respect to food. Thus, we shall return to the explanations in the last chapter. There, the main question was how and to what degree can humans regulate land use on Earth, i.e. regulate the blue and green water flow, and whether by this they route the precipitation into the atmosphere or into the rivers. It was shown that land use is changed in order to produce food such as grain, vegetables, and meat. The growth of crops and thus our food is secured by the green water flow of plant transpiration.

We should put the discussion of blue and green water flow on hold for a moment and look at the question of how much water is needed to cover our daily calorie intake. Initially, we can ignore where the water comes from.

In preparation of the World Food Summit in 1996, the Food and Agriculture Organization of the UN (FAO), produced a simple yet lucid estimate that I would like to present below. The FAO assumed that all people on Earth have the food available that they need for a healthy life. With a balanced diet and average physical activity, humans need approximately 3000 kcal per day. The FAO states that a balanced diet consists of 2400 kcal per day of plant products and 600 kcal per day of animal products. For at least a generation, this percentage of animal products seems to be too low by average Central European standards, because we have become used to much more meat on our plates. However, since this high percentage is not a requirement for a balanced diet, I would prefer to stay with the FAO assumption.

Table 4 has shown us that through the transpiration coefficient, the green water flow is directly linked to building up the dry mass of vegetation. However, the amount of dry mass produced does not correspond to the ultimate amount of food produced. First, the leftover plant material from the harvest, i.e. stalks, thorns, and leaves must be subtracted. They count as biomass that was built up from CO_2. However, they cannot be digested by humans. This leftover plant material makes up the major part of the harvest. For normal crops, this amounts to two-thirds of

Crop	GreenWaterConsumption [1/kg]	GreenWaterConsumption [1/1000kcal]
Wheat flour	1500	470
Tubers	700	780
Sugar plants	150	490
Legumes	1900	550
Oil plants	2000	730
Vegetable oil	2000	230
Vegetables	500	2070
Average		530

Table 10 Green water use to produce various selected crops in liters per kilogram of food (column 2) and liters per 1000 kilocalories (column 3).

the biomass produced. Thus, the actual harvest is only one-third of the biomass. Therefore, the crop needs three times the amount of water, in order to grow, for example, one kilogram of wheat flour. This amount is approximately 1500 liters of evaporation water (FAO, 1999). Thus, one of the goals of plant breeding was and is to reduce the percentage of leftover plant material after the harvest in relation to the grain yield and thus improve the water efficiency of the plants. High-yield strains of wheat now achieve a grain percentage of over 50% of the total harvested biomass, which is a yield index of more than 50%.

Table 10 gives the water usage of selected plants. This table shows the amount of water that must evaporate in order to produce 1000 kcal of food. As mentioned above, in order to produce for example 1 kg of wheat flour, 1500 liters of evaporation water are needed. With a nutritional value of 3200 kcal per kilogram for wheat flour, 470 liters of evaporation water are needed to produce 1000 kcal of food. If the different categories of crops are compared, it is noticeable that there are large differences in the amount of water needed by the crops. For instance, 1000 kcal-worth of vegetable oil can be produced for 230 liters of water, while 1000 calories of vegetables use over 2000 liters of water. As can be seen in the last row of Table 10, an average of approximately 500 liters of evaporation water is needed to produce 1000 kcal of crops. Therefore, in order to obtain the 2400 kcal that humans should have daily from crops, 1200 liters of evaporation water must be used each day.

If we continue with the FAO assumptions, the production of 1000 kcal of animal products as meat needs 4000 liters of evaporation water. Thus, the amount of water that is needed to produce the equivalent amount of meat is eight times as much as the water needed to produce grain. And this average value adopted by the FAO is quite optimistic. As a matter of fact, this low value can only be obtained by keeping the animals in pens. In this case, the space in which the animals can move freely is rather limited. Thus the animals have the optimal external conditions for gaining weight and converting their feed into large amounts of milk and meat. Free-range animals need much larger amounts of green water due to their freedom of movement and also possible heat and cold stress. In this case, up to 17,000 liters are needed for 1000 calories of meat.

Why is there this glaring difference in the use of green water between growing crops and raising animals for meat? The raw product for the production of meat is vegetation. The vegetation is consumed by the animals and delivers the major part of the energy necessary to sustain the animal's life. Only a small part, about 10%, of the energy contained in the feed contributes to the animal's growth and thus goes into the meat. Thus, due to the lower water requirements of fodder plants, for the production of 600 kcal of meat, 2400 liters of green water are needed daily.

A total of approximately 3600 liters per day or respectively 1300 m³/a of water is needed to ensure that one person has a healthy, balanced diet. This is, as the genesis of this figure showed, quite a simplified yet realistic estimate of the green water flow which should be available for all people to ensure their food supply.

What does this figure mean? If we compare this 3600 liters per day with the minimal amount of water needed for drinking and sanitation as well as industrial uses of 160 liters per day, the water that humans need to ensure their food supply seems exorbitantly large. We need approximately twenty-five times the amount of water to ensure our food supply as to ensure our basic hygiene needs. Even more serious is the fact that the water needed for our food supply differs fundamentally from the water used for drinking and sanitation. This is due to the fact that all possible ways that could further expand the capacity of the agrarian production system through clever multiple use of green water are blocked. As a basic principle, the same water cannot be used for evaporation twice. This is in contrast to blue water, in which through clever coordination, can be used almost as often as it is needed.

How realistic is this simplified FAO estimate? Gleick (2000) carried out a far more comprehensive investigation on the status of the Earth's water resources and their connection with the world's food supply. He did not assume how much water a person needed for a balanced diet, but rather how much food was actually produced and how it was consumed. In doing so, he took the different dietary habits in different regions into account. He came to the conclusion that the actual average water use for the production of food is around 1200 m³ per person per year. This means that today, the world population of the planet uses an amount of water that is quite close to that needed for a balanced diet.

Is everything all right then? Firstly good news: in principle, already today enough green water is used worldwide to feed the Earth's entire population. Therefore, the Earth has the necessary amount of green water at its disposal. However, nothing has been said about the degree of sustainability of the current usages of water resources. And now the bad news: if the green water flow used for the food supply is considered more exactly, there are large regional differences. Whereas North Americans use 1800 m³ and Europeans use 1600 m³ per person per year to ensure their food supply, parts of Africa and Asia use only 600 to 900 m³ per person per year. Thus, the worldwide average suggests a green water flow for food production that only seems satisfactory.

6.5 Water and lifestyles

These large differences in water use between the industrialized and the developing countries are the result of differences in diet. Whereas meat is around 30–35% of the daily calorie intake in the industrialized countries and drives the green water consumption up, the low figures in the poorest developing countries indicate that the calorie intake of the population is too low. There are approximately 800 million malnourished people concealed behind the bare figure of 600–900 m³ evaporation water per person per year in these regions. Thus, in the developing countries, water use for food production must be increased. In order to achieve the target for global water consumption needed to ensure a healthy diet of at least 1300 m³ evaporation water per person per year, it is self-evident that the developed countries in North America and Europe have to reduce their food-production water use and thus change their food patterns in the

	Human water consumption in m³ per person per year			
	Targeted		Actual	
	Developing countries	Industrial countries	Average	Range
Food	1300	1600	1200	600–1800
Household	40	40	30	20–40
Industries	130	130	130	10–140
Total	1470	1760	1360	630–1980

Table 11   Actual and targeted human water consumption of the populations of the developing and industrial countries (after Falkenmark, 2004)

future. There is evidence that this has already started to happen. In many countries in Europe, the calorie intake of the population is gradually decreasing. Furthermore, meat consumption in Western Europe is also decreasing. This trend is based on the increasing consciousness of health problems caused by too much meat in our diets. However, these first, vague signs of a reduction in water use for food production cannot lead us to believe that it will decrease from the present 1700 m³ per person per year to the desired 1300 m³ anytime soon. In fact, it would be more realistic to strive for water consumption figures of 1300 m³ per person per year for the developing countries and 1600 m³ for the developed countries, as shown in Table 11.

The table shows human water consumption in two columns. It is differentiated between the water consumption that humans need for a healthy, hygienic life, independent of where they live, and current water consumption. The last column shows that the actual human water consumption in the different regions of the planet can vary by a factor of three. This is solely due to the different lifestyles that people lead in different cultures and the water resources used for food production.

The relatively simple deliberations of the FAO on water needs for a healthy, balanced diet lead to a basic water consumption for humans of 1300 m^3 per person per year. The FAO already assumed that a sign of a healthy diet is a balance between plant and animal products. Both a purely vegetarian or purely non-vegetarian diet are seen as unrealistic in international deliberations. Besides the differences in lifestyles, which are abundant in connection to this topic, particularly in our culture, in the analysis of the necessary amount of water to provide a balanced diet, one fact becomes very clear: in a best-case scenario, the production of meat still requires three times as much water as to produce the same amount of vegetation and in a worst-case scenario, meat production requires seventeen times as much.

Therefore, our menus determine the amount of water used.

How great is the range of the amount of water used due to the differences in diet and lifestyles? The minimum amount of water used corresponds to a purely vegetarian diet. Here, it is possible to produce 3000 kcal per day with only 550 m^3 per person per year, which is after all only 42% of the recommended amount of 1300 m^3 per person per year. Thus, it would be possible to halve the present water consumption by converting the world's population into vegetarians. This would allow (purely theoretically) the doubling of the world's population. This could put us in an optimistic mood.

Maximum water consumption, on the other hand, means that 40–50% of the daily calorie intake comes from meat. This essentially corresponds to the wishful thinking of the majority of humans. In America, Australia, and Europe, we dream of big, plate-sized sirloin steaks from free-range cattle that graze in the wide open ranges, often spiced up with a bit of Wild West romanticism. In Southeast Asia they dream of daily Peking duck and in the Middle East it is a luscious daily ration of succulent lamb. An exception are the people of India: to a large extent, their menu is traditionally vegetarian.

A simple calculation shows a green water use of 12,000 m³ per person per year for a diet that is rich in meat. This is twenty-four times the amount for a purely vegetarian diet and ten times the water consumption assumed by the FAO.

I freely admit that I have chosen a diet rich in meat. And I do not have to feel like I am eccentric, because in the large-scale field test that was carried out in recent years in the industrialized countries, the majority of the population made a similar choice. Due to the rise in income in the industrialized countries during the second half of the 20th century, for the first time in history eating meat was no longer a question of income. The majority of the population decided on a diet rich in meat and thus, for a lifestyle that needed a large amount of green water. This is made particularly clear if we look how hamburgers have conquered menus worldwide in the past fifty years. A hamburger is the leit-motif of a diet that is rich in meat. No other recipe has ever been more successful. It is approximately 20 g bun and, originally, a meat patty with about 100 g of beef. For the most part, the calo-ries come from the meat. At the request of the customers, the meat patty in modern hamburgers is now even larger and is still increasing. It appears that a further increase in the size of the meat patty is limited only by the static properties of the burger and thus the ability to eat it.

For now, let's stay with the original hamburger in its classi-cal form. To produce the 20 g bun, around 20 liters of water are needed. In Germany, the production of the 100 g meat patty requires, depending on the type of animal husbandry practiced, between 3500 and 7000 liters of green water. Extensive pasturing

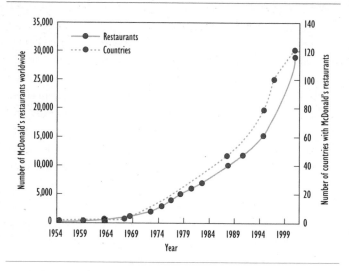

Figure 26 Development of the number of McDonald's restaurants and
countries with McDonald's restaurants since 1954

in South America requires even more water. This example shows
more than any other how lifestyle dominates the use of the
Earth's green water resources. So, the next time you eat a hamburger, imagine the thirty-five virtual bathtubs filled with water
that you are consuming.

As an indicator of the hamburger's conquest of the globe,
Fig. 26 shows the increase in the number of McDonald's restaurants in the last fifty years as well as the sharp increase in
the number of countries that have McDonald's restaurants. This
curve is much steeper than the slope of the population curve.
This fast-food restaurant chain was able to double its numbers
between 1995 and 2003, which is only eight years.

Fig. 26 is striking not only because of the massive increase in the number of McDonald's restaurants in the last fifty years, but also the increase in the number of countries that offer this kind of food, now up to 120. And it seems that existing cultural borders were broken through without any difficulty. In most of the countries, the food supply in the fast-food chains is essentially based on beef. The trend shown in Fig. 26 should not be taken as the Americanization of the world's food, but rather as a sign of the desire for diets richer in meat and as a first sign that prosperity is increasing worldwide and not just in the industrialized countries. However, in some countries, for example India, foreign fast-food chains offer predominantly or even exclusively vegetarian fare, due to pressure from government.

6.6 Summary

The water requirements for humans are now clear and we can note the following:

1   Drinking water and water for sanitation are not in short supply. Water quality means quality of life, which can be produced for all people with 20 to 40 liters of water per day.
2   The major part of water consumption is used in producing food. There is worldwide agreement as to what constitutes an adequate and healthy diet, which needs to have 1300 m³ of water available per person per year. The Earth system is capable of delivering this amount for everyone alive today, but the food produced with this water is not distributed fairly among the planet's population.
3   Man-made water consumption is essentially determined by our diet and thus through our lifestyle and pattern of consumption. This suggests that we can choose our

own individual water consumption. However, we often forget that this holds for only a small part of the world's population. The rest have to eat what is available and there is too often too little available. Nevertheless, experience has shown that when humans are able to choose the level of water consumption they require for their diet, they generally choose the higher end of the consumption scale, in that they choose a diet rich in meat.

Therefore, we should keep our eye on the green water flow. Here is where shortages might occur due to the increasing need for food and the current, already quite high degree of utilization. Humans will decide about the further use of the green water flow according to their income, value system, and immediate demands. Are there mechanisms by which the imbalance in the use of the water resources on Earth, as discussed in the last chapter, can be reduced? Are there ways to determine how much water the Earth has left for us? These are the questions that I will cover in the next chapter, before we take a look at the future in the final chapter.

7 Virtual Water

There is a lot of water in our food. However, water is also used in producing our food. This amount of "indirect" water exceeds the weight of the food produced by a factor of 1000 to 50,000. In addition, the manufacture of goods also uses water, with weight relationships that are often similar. According to investigations by Williams (2002), the production of a memory chip that weighs 2 g, such as used in computers, requires 32,000 g of water.

The Earth's life-support system already provides the world's population with green water flow to produce food. The actual problem is the disproportionate regional distribution of the green water flow and thus the occurrence of surpluses and deficits.

How can this global imbalance be corrected and thus end water scarcity in deficit regions? In principle, there are two possibilities:

1   The surplus, unused water is exported from the water-rich regions to the water-poor regions where it is used to produce food. This has already been done in certain cases. For many years, the major part of the flow of the Colorado River in the American West is pumped by massive pumping stations through large pipelines over the Rocky Mountains to California, where it is used for irrigation and as drinking water. The Colorado River collects the precipitation and meltwater of the eastern Rocky Mountains and as little

as a hundred years ago, it used to drain as a broad river into the Gulf of California. Currently, it rarely reaches the ocean because so much water is diverted that the river runs dry before it gets there. However, the high technical effort and energy costs due to the pumping generally make transporting irrigation water a very unprofitable enterprise. In addition, large amounts of water cannot be transported across continents.

2 The surplus water in the water-rich regions is used to produce water-intensive goods that are exported. Exporting water-intensive goods reduces the amount of water transported by a factor of 1000 to 50,000. Thus, it is much more profitable than exporting water itself. If an economy exports a water-intensive product such as meat or memory chips to another country, then it is exporting in an abstract way the water which was used to produce the goods. While the water is used for the export, it is not itself exported.

The water in Example 2 above is called "virtual" water. The concept of virtual water was introduced in the early 1990s by Tony Allan (Allan, 1993). With virtual water, the use of water resources can be taken into consideration in the production and export of goods. It is important, especially for water-scarce regions, to calculate how the available amount of water can be best utilized. For example, in arid regions, is it better to concentrate on generating and exporting renewable energy from the abundant solar energy found there and to use that money to import water-intensive products, or is it better to try and produce these goods at home and run the risk of misusing scarce water or using it too expensively or even worse having to import water to do it?

The concept of virtual water is very helpful for comparing the cost-benefit ratios of different strategies in the future. It allows the water to be traced throughout the world and through its entire use cycle from precipitation to manufacturing goods to evaporation and to the use of the goods up to their disposal.

7.1 What is virtual water?

Virtual water is the water that is embedded in a product. If we look at one kilogram of flour, then we are not talking about the actual water content of the flour, but rather the amount of water that is needed to produce that flour. In our terms, this is the 1500 liters of evaporation water that has already been mentioned. The concept of virtual water combines green and blue water, because here it no longer matters whether the water flow is green or blue. With virtual water it is important to realize that it represents a specific amount of the natural resource used for a specific purpose. The same amount of virtual water cannot be used for another purpose. Thus, it is not possible to use the virtual water, which is embedded in our kilogram of flour, to create another kilogram of flour or forty-five microchips. In this respect, virtual water cannot be arbitrarily increased. Thus, the virtual water that is imported into a country should be added to the water resources in that country, in order to find out to what extent the country utilizes the Earth's water resources. Thus, when Germany, as is often the case, imports large amounts of Mediterranean citrus fruits in the winter, the German consumer is utilizing the water resources of those countries. We are importing virtual water that was evaporated in these countries for our purposes and which can no longer be used for any other purpose. On the other hand, if the same consumers manufacture microchips in Germany with the country's own water resources and then export the chips to the Mediterranean, the amount of virtual water is balanced again.

In order to be able to use the concept of virtual water in the future as an instrument for the better distribution of Earth's water resources, let's take another step.

We can ask ourselves how much water would be used if the desired product, here in our example the equivalent of one kilogram of grain, were to be produced where the demand for it exists. This approach asks how much water could be saved if the product was produced in the country and not imported. This is the crucial question for water-scarce countries. It is the starting-point of every deliberation as to how the water can be used most efficiently on a global scale.

However, there is a problem with this concept of virtual water. What happens when a product is imported into a country in which it cannot be produced? For example, in Germany, rice cannot be grown due to the climate. As a result, the virtual water content of rice could not be determined for Germany. In order to be able to determine it despite this, a suitable product needs to be found that could substitute for the rice. This homegrown product should be similar to rice in composition and nutritional value and be able to be substituted for rice in the diet. If the virtual water in the equivalent amount of rice is less than the amount of virtual water needed to produce the substitute, then for the protection of worldwide water resources, it is better to import rice into Germany and conserve water resources here. In this sense, we could even come to the paradoxical conclusion that saltwater fish from the ocean contain virtual water, although these fish never use fresh water resources. All that matters is that they can be substituted for food products produced with fresh water, because they contain nutrients such as protein.

This concept of virtual water allows us, at least in principle, to investigate all traded goods for the amount of water used to produce them and how far they can be substituted by equivalent goods that need less water. Thus, this provides us with the first tool to counter the somewhat depressing conclusions from the last chapter, which dealt with issues of lifestyles, water consumption, hunger, and surplus. With this tool we do not have to accept these conclusions as unchangeable. At the end of this global site analysis, it should be clear, what food and which industrial products can be produced where using the least amount of virtual water. The results of these analyses can then be employed to use water resources more efficiently and distribute them more fairly.

When the concept of virtual water is used to trace the path that water takes through different products in agricultural and industrial production, it should not stop when the product, i.e. the orange leaves the grove or the microchip leaves the factory. A consistent consideration of water paths includes the entire life-cycle of the product. It considers transport to the customer, the environmental impact that the product has during and after its use, the possibility of re-using or recycling the product and quantifies the amount of water used as well as the amount of water needed to dispose of the product, and in its final decomposition. Only such an integrated consideration of a product's use of the water resources allows the most economical use of water.

The analysis of the global water flow in the course of a product's life cycle is a fascinating and new way of considering the use of our natural resources. It is still in its infancy, but it consistently follows the guidelines of the Dublin Principles on Water and Sustainable Development. The ability to use this tool is a prerequisite for sustainable use of this resource.

What are the practical benefits of the concept of virtual water?

An essential benefit is that virtual water can be traded. This

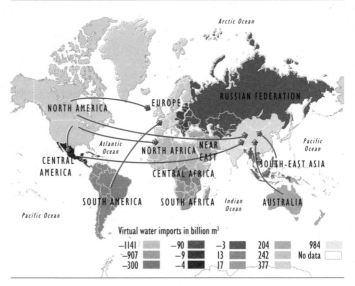

Figure 27 Worldwide trade with virtual water in billion km³ per year
(after Hoekstra, 2000)

should serve to secure water reserves and to ensure a more efficient use of water resources.

Fig. 27 shows a first estimate of the virtual water flow on Earth.
The regions where the arrows start are net exporters of virtual
water and the regions to which they point are net importers. As
net exporters, North and South America as well as Australia and
New Zealand stand out. This is because they are major exporters
of meat. Russia has balanced virtual water, while China, North
Africa, and Europe are major importers of virtual water, due to
their importation of meat and grain. The total amount of the
virtual water that is involved in the international trade in food
was 1340 km³ in 2000, which, after all, is already more than 1%

of the total precipitation on the land surface or more than 3% of the human-regulated green water flow (see Table 6). Crops make up 60% of the trade in virtual water, 14% is fish and seafood, 13% is animal products excepting meat, and 13% is meat.

Importing virtual water reduces the pressure on limited water resources and can therefore, especially in water-scarce countries, contribute to defusing water conflicts and preventing possible wars. Virtual water is generally better suited to do this than a newly-discovered spring or a newly tapped fossil groundwater aquifer, because the water-intensive food imported is produced in the country of origin under much more sustainable conditions than would be possible by using the non-sustainable springs and aquifers in the water-scarce regions threatened by conflict.

The economic dimension follows the political dimension. The concept of virtual water ensures that countries export the goods that they are able to produce more favorably than their competitors, while they import goods that they cannot produce more favorably. In this sense, introducing trade in virtual water would make a new instrument available that could improve the efficiency of global water use via market mechanisms. In a global economic system, it makes sense to concentrate water-intensive production in areas where water is available in surplus. Water is cheap in these regions, it can be sustainably collected as precipitation and does not have to be extracted from non-renewable sources, such as fossil groundwater, and in general, it does not have to be transported long distances. In addition, in many cases, less water is needed to produce a specific product than in regions where water is scarce. The trade with virtual water between a region, in which the efficiency of water use is high and a region where it low, and this is the decisive point, leads to *real* water savings.

How large are these savings at present? For the year 2000,

estimates from Oki *et al.* (2003) are available that come to the conclusion that trading virtual water could save 455 km³ of water. Since these savings are mainly due to having prevented irrigation by trade, the conclusion can be drawn that international trade with virtual water could save every fifth cubic-meter of irrigation water.

Thus, trading with virtual water between nations and between regions within nations can be an alternative to the expensive transfer of blue water. Demands for transporting blue water beyond catchment-area boundaries and its use as irrigation water, as described for the Colorado River in the USA, are becoming louder. At present, China is planning a gigantic network of canals and pumping stations to divert water from the Yangtze River in the humid south to agricultural areas of the drier north. Here it should be checked whether it would make more economic sense to use the water resources in the south to grow the crops there and to deliver them to the north than to transport the water over the mountains.

Speaking more generally, the key question is whether it would make more sense both economically and ecologically to build a large number of smaller dams to store water in times of high precipitation and thus high water resource availability, in order to produce the largest possible amount of food, which could be then stored for use in times of food scarcity, instead of building a few large dams to store the water over long periods of time, so that food can also be produced in times of water scarcity.

Already today, virtual water is being stored in global food reserves. If the total virtual water that is stockpiled in the strategic reserves of grain, sugar, meat, and vegetable oil were to be added together, it would fill a virtual lake with a volume of 830 km³. That is approximately 14% of the water contained in all of the real dams on the planet put together. If we add the virtual water stored in herds of cattle and sheep, the total virtual water currently stored on Earth would have a volume of 4600 km³. That is a formidable 77% of the volume of all reservoirs on Earth. These amounts show that virtual water has become a considerable reservoir. It has reached a size that would allow it to alleviate worldwide temporary water crises and defuse potential conflicts.

For the first time, the concept of virtual water ensures the global traceability of the use of a natural resource throughout the entire life cycle of products, in this case food. Thus, it provides the first chance to evaluate man's utilization of the services of the Earth's life-support system. This is connected to the possibility of trading these services. This again opens up the possibility of using market mechanisms not only to work towards the political goal of sustainable use of water resources, but also actually to achieve it.

7.2 Combining consumption and environmental sustainability: The Water Footprint

The virtual water in a product tells us something about the utilization of the services of Earth's life-support system in its production. Due to the increasing world population and rising prosperity, in the coming decades the demand for goods that have been produced with the use of water, most of all food, will increase sharply. Thus, the question arises as to whether there is a maximum amount of virtual water. In other words, where is the limit to utilizing the services of Earth's life-support system that are connected with water?

At first, this question appears difficult to answer, because it is very academic and abstract. However, the question how long our water will last is at the very heart of this book.

How do we start to answer such a question? I would like to try and develop the answer through the basic principles of coexistence between humans and nature.

Every person needs land to live on. This fundamental service of the Earth system comes long before water and food are delivered. Thus, a surface, or as we say, "land," is a natural resource. However, land is not the same type of natural resource as water or oxygen. Unlike both of these, land is not renewable, is not part of a cycle, and cannot be increased or enlarged.

All water-based services of the life-support system, for example the provision of drinking or sanitation water, food production, waste removal, and sewage disposal are also bound to a specific surface area, on which the biological and chemical processes that they are based on can take place. When humans utilize these services, they leave an imaginary footprint upon the land surface. This footprint is as large as the area that is needed to satisfy the demand for these services system *sustainably*. This area is called the water footprint of an individual or community.

Thus, a certain area is needed for food production, another for decomposition of waste, another to treat the sewage water, etc. These areas add up to our water footprint. If we live a life that uses our natural resources intensively, for example if we eat a lot of beef, then we utilize a larger green water flow and thus a larger area on which the Earth system sustainably supplies it, than if we were vegetarians. The water footprints of all people add up to one large water footprint for mankind. If the area of the footprint exceeds the area of the surface of the Earth, then the point has been reached at which the existence of mankind can no longer be ensured sustainably by the planet's life-support system. Safeguarding mankind's existence is thus inevitably connected to damage to the Earth system due to over-use. Thus, the water footprint concept allows us to answer the question, based on the ultimately fixed land surface, when the utilization of water resources will no longer be sustainable.

The water footprint, and its determination using virtual water, is very similar to the concept of the ecological footprint (Wackernagel and Rees, 1996). Currently, there are only a few significant studies on the ecological footprint and almost none on the human water footprint, which determine the area required through use of water-based services. I would like to present an example here, which deals with the water footprint of an individual in a riparian country of the Baltic Sea. In the foreground is the question as to when the point is reached, due to the man-made impact in the natural cycle of matter in the catchment area of Baltic Sea, at which the integrity of the life-support system is impaired. Jansson et. al. (1999) have provided such a study on the approximate population of 85 million in this catchment area. They analyzed the land and water resources that the population of the area uses in order to uphold its present living conditions and habits of consumption.

With Jansson's method, the determination of the water footprint begins with the analysis of the virtual water content of the goods that a person consumes and the services they use. Next, the amount of virtual water needed is converted to the equivalent areas. This is relatively simple for the green water flow that is needed for the production of one kilogram of flour. We already saw earlier that on average, a person needs a green water flow of 1300 m³ per year for a healthy diet. The transpiration flow through plants and thus the productive green water flow is about 260 liters per square meter per year for the Baltic catchment area. Thus, for the necessary transpiration flow of about 1300 m³ per year, a person in this area must have approximately 4800 m² available for the green water flow.

The area needed for other services can be determined similarly. Areas are needed for the wood to grow on that is used for fuel and for a newspaper or for building a house, or for the disposal of waste that is treated in rivers and lakes. The sum of these areas is the water footprint of an individual who lives in this catchment area. On the whole, the analyses that must be carried out to determine the water footprint are complex. However, in their integrated approach, they closely follow the guiding principles of the Dublin Statement on water and sustainable development. Not all of these methods have been sufficiently perfected yet for this approach to be used for a worldwide inventory of the regional capacity of the Earth system. The main problem lies in the determination of the long-term efficiency and capacity of the processes involved in sustainable food production, energy generation, and waste disposal and water treatment. At present, we can definitely say that it is quite possible to create short-term increases in agricultural yield through massive use of artificial fertilizers. However, it is still unclear how long these yield increases can be continued without irreversibly damaging the soil or destabilizing the ecosystem by reducing biological diversity.

The result of Jansson's research for an average resident of the Baltic catchment area is shown in Fig. 28. Five different Earth system services were considered: provision of drinking and industrial water, provision of food (carbohydrates, fats, and animal and plant protein), provision of wood products (paper, houses, fuel, etc.), decomposition of waste that is disposed of in the lakes, and decomposition of waste that are disposed of in the rivers and then transported away. Firstly, the area that is needed to perform each service is analyzed. The precipitation that falls in the Baltic Sea region, on an area of 440 m^2, is sufficient to provide, at the present consumption habits, the drinking and

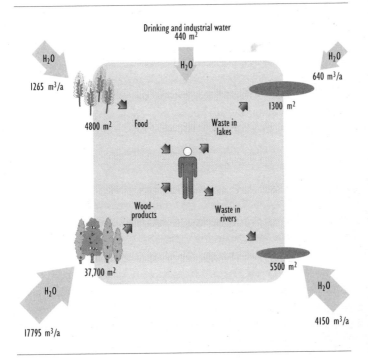

Figure 28   The water footprint of a resident of a Baltic Sea riparian
            country, expressed in area required to provide the respective
            service of the Earth system (gray area) as well as green (left)
            and blue (right) water flow through the Baltic catchment area
            (after Jansson, 1999)

gray water, as well as the industrial water for a resident. Food
production requires, as already illustrated above, an area of 4800
m² or almost half a hectare. To provide the wood products consumed for heating, house-building, newspapers, etc., a biomass
growth of an area of 37,700 m² is necessary and for the sustainable natural treatment of waste, a lake area of 1300 m² and river

area of 5600 m^2 are necessary. Added together, a resident of this catchment area, with their present lifestyle, requires an area of 50,000 m^2, or five hectares, in order to be *sustainably* supplied with the necessary water-supported services of the Earth system. This area represents the amount of water that must be moved as either green or blue water on each respective area through-out a year in order to provide the respective services. These are represented by the arrows in Fig. 28. They indicate the amounts of used blue and green water respectively. Since the designated area can only be used by one person, this model allows a simple yet realistic evaluation of the entire use of the water-supported services of the Earth system.

The water footprint of a Baltic Sea resident shown in Fig. 28 contains astoundingly high amounts of green water, especially in the consumption of wood. This is primarily due to the energy consumption of burning wood for heating. However, most of the inhabitants of the Baltic do not burn wood to heat their homes, but use fossil fuels, which are not sustainable. In order to determine the water consumption and thus the area required that would be necessary if a resident of this area were to operate sustainably, the wood consumption necessary to replace the fossil fuels currently used was determined. In this way, crude oil, as for the saltwater fish described above, also has virtual water embedded in it. The same is true for the high consumption of wood to make paper for newspapers as well as wood used for building homes.

The interesting question now is whether the catchment area of the Baltic Sea is sufficient to sustainably provide all the resi-dents, with their present lifestyle, with the water-supported services that they need. Or is their present standard of living unavoidably unsustainable?

A simple extrapolation leads to the astounding result that the area required is more than two times the size of the Baltic

Sea catchment area. If, as described above, every resident needs five hectares of land to operate sustainably, with 85 million residents that results in a total required area of about 4.25 million km². However, the catchment area of the Baltic Sea is only 1.75 million km². Thus, this example clearly shows that the residents of this area cannot maintain their lifestyles and their consumption habits sustainably solely from the water resources available in their territory. Thus, they are dependent upon the import of virtual water and thus upon Earth-system services that were originally created in other countries, or they must rely on services that are not sustainable. For the most part, the imports to cover the service gaps are non-renewable fossil fuels such as natural gas, crude oil, or coal. Thus, at the expense of sustainability, the large areas that would be needed for wood products can be reduced considerably, indeed to such an extent that that Baltic Sea countries can even export large quantities of wood.

The required area shown in Fig. 28, based on water-supported sustainable services, is not invariable. It is the result of specific lifestyles and consumption habits. If, for example, home insulation was improved or the newspapers were read on the internet, thus not requiring paper, the area required for wood products would decrease. Reducing the amount of wood used by half and thus halving the corresponding area required would lead to a decrease in the total area needed per person by about three hectares. An increase in beef consumption could rapidly increase the area needed, easily doubling it. This would not be true however, if instead of beef, Baltic Sea fish were mainly chosen as food. Fish would provide quite a bit of virtual water, without straining the water resources on land. The use of sewage treatment plants would also reduce the area needed to dispose of the waste in rivers and lakes. In addition, the use of electricity generated by water power, i.e. sustainably, for heating homes would reduce the forest area needed.

These examples could be expanded almost at will. They show that the size of our water footprint is not just dependent upon our lifestyles or daily habits, but also on the use of the right technologies and the intelligent handling of water and thus can be organized to a considerable extent.

8 The Future of our Water Resources

It is now time to return to the beginning of this book, where we looked at Fig. 1 and saw the predictions from the International Water Management Institute (IMWI) in Sri Lanka on the future of the Earth's water resources. According to them, in 2025, wide regions of the planet will suffer from either economical or physical water scarcity. Economic water scarcity means that there are no surplus water resources and thus economic considerations must be also taken into account. Already a large number of countries will suffer this in 2025 and will be forced to import food, i.e. virtual water, from other countries. Physical water scarcity is defined by the IMWI as being if more than 40% of the available blue water is used for the production of food and thus diverted into green water flow. Experience has shown that after this threshold has been passed, water conflicts, triggered by water scarcity, force the population to resort on a massive scale to unsustainable practices such as exploiting fossil groundwater.

At first it is not surprising that those regions that will be affected by physical water scarcity in the future are consistently found in the driest areas on the planet. The majority of the population does not live there and are thus not directly affected. Against the background of the discussion on virtual water, the worldwide trade in food and the globalization of markets, does the IMWI's map evaluate the water resources and their scarcity incorrectly?

First of all, water resources are still fundamentally the precipitation that falls upon the continents. Only this amount of
water is continually renewed and can thus be used sustainably.
Therefore we know that our water resources will still last a very
long time. No sensible climate scenario has ever been calculated
that resulted, like in a biblical apocalypse, in a complete end of
precipitation on Earth. However, the options for using our water
resources to produce goods and services, especially food, are
becoming increasingly restricted. Correspondingly, the competition between humans and nature for water resources is becoming
more and more severe.

This sounds as if two opponents are fighting. If this were the
case, humans would be fighting against their own life-support
system. From a global perspective, this would be comparable
to a serious autoimmune disease in which the immune system
destroys its own body. Generally, this ends fatally for both parties,
the person and the immune system. Thus, such a battle would be
a lose-lose situation.

As we have seen, we can now specify the limit up to which
humans can still use the water services of the Earth system sustainably, but we still cannot truly quantify it: it is reached when
the sum of all the water footprints of all people on Earth exceed
the area of the continents. Are we heading towards this point?
How far away are we from it?

We are, as Jill Jäger (2007) described in detail in her book
in this series, *Our Planet: How Much More Can Earth Take?*,
faced with an eventful, but not hopeless future. We have 300
years of unprecedented, uncontrolled growth behind us. This
created unprecedented knowledge, developed breakthrough
technologies, and accumulated tremendous riches. However, for
the first time, they have also shown us the limits that Earth holds
in store. By now, the Earth system no longer reacts just in small

ways, but also as a whole to mankind's attempts to take over the matter cycles. One thing is clear: there is neither enough room nor enough resources available on Earth to allow further growth in the same way as the last 300 years. Thus, we are inevitably faced with far-reaching changes.

What do we know and what do we suspect that the future will bring? Climate change will continue climate researchers' computer models will draw up images of the future climate with increasing reliability. The Earth will become between 2–5°C warmer than now and, much more important for water resources, the precipitation will also change. In the upcoming century, global warming in the tropics will be comparatively low, whereas at the poles and in the tundra and taiga of Siberia and Canada, it could be over 10°C. In the latter regions, this will trigger far-reaching changes, particularly if the mean annual temperature rises above freezing-point. In that case, the frozen soils of the permafrost will melt. This will lead to changes in the vegetation in these regions and the vegetation will be able to penetrate further into the thawed soil. In our latitudes, it is foreseeable that winter precipitation will increase in the future, whereas summer precipitation will decrease. Thus, with increasing temperatures, the climate of Northern Europe will become more like the Mediterranean.

Everything indicates that precipitation will become more extreme. Places that have little rain nowadays will receive even less rain and places that already have a lot, will get even more. Thus, droughts will become more severe and floods worse. How the precipitation distribution on Earth will change in detail in the course of the expected climate changes, whether the precipitation on the continents will increase or decrease, and what effects this will have upon water resources, are all part of today's most fascinating questions in climate and water research. In these fields all of the complex feedback mechanisms between vegetation and the greenhouse gases, between humans and land use, between the oceans and the continents, must be taken into account. All indications are that the expected changes in the total precipitation on the continents will not be too dramatic. However, this does not rule out that drastic changes in precipitation could occur in various regions, such as Southern Europe, the savannas of the African Sahel, Southern Africa, and the monsoon areas of Asia.

In its 2001 report, the Intergovernmental Panel on Climate Change (IPCC) noted that "regional climate changes already influence hydrological systems as well as terrestrial and marine ecosystems" and that the "increasing socio-economical damages that are now linked to these regional climate variations, indicate an increasing vulnerability with respect to Global Change." Above all, this increased vulnerability will in turn create an "increasing health threat, especially in that part of the population with low income and in the countries of the tropics and subtropics."

At first, these statements sound quite vague. Measured against the fact that the IPCC is an independent panel of leading scientists from around the world, who had to agree on the formulation of a common statement, it is quite clear. It means climate change has already begun, it is already influencing water systems, there is no indication that it will improve life on Earth, it is already costing money, and it will probably cost much more in the future.

In the future much more will change than just the climate. There are important developments, whose course during the next fifty years, and also to some extent for the next 100 years, can already be estimated. An example of this is the further increase in population. As already described, mankind's strategy as a life form is to continually increase the number of individuals. However, for about thirty years now – which in relation to the three billion years of Earth's history is comparable to a milli-second in a day – this strategy has been changing. There is no doubt now that in the "foreseeable" future, which is still longer than a generation, the number of people on Earth will stabilize. This development has started and it will start to show effects in the next few decades.

Today, the annual population growth rate is 1.2%. That means an additional 78 million people must be taken care of each year. In the year 2050, and this estimate is almost certain, the population of the world will be around 9.5 billion people, but the annual growth rate will only be 0.5%. That means that "only" an additional 48 million people must be taken care of each year. If this trend continues, the population of the world will stabilize in about 2075 at approximately 11 billion people and will then start to decrease.

This development is astounding. It is all the more so if we observe that in many parts of the world, excepting China for the most part, this is not the result of government compulsion. In fact, many people decide of their own free will, if they have the choice, the education, and a certain level of prosperity, to not procreate at the same rate. This is mainly the result of two developments:

1   More education and information that make it believable that prosperity can, or can *only* be achieved by having fewer children.
2   More freedom for women to participate in deciding how many children they want. Above all, this also includes the increased use of birth control worldwide for married couples.

Overall, the presumed moderate changes in amounts of

precipitation, the efforts to limit the increase of atmospheric CO_2 as well as the deceleration of population growth are good news for water resources. In his book *Climate Change: The Point of No Return* (2007), in this series, Mojib Latif describes very definite courses of action that would ensure that we could stabilize the climate through sustainability. Together with the positive population development they provide hope that the growth from the last 300 years will not continue unhindered and that we are already preparing a soft landing. What could such a landing be like? And where would we land?

In addition to the dominant factor of increasing population, in particular future lifestyles and the technologies used will decide where we will land, how soft the landing will be, and how sustainably we will use water resources.

As we have seen already, this is not really a matter of drinking, sanitation, or industrial water. These can, assuming corresponding political will, be made available to all people at high quality with comparatively little financial expenditure and without damaging the Earth system. They will not be exhausted so quickly. The challenge for the future sustainable use of the water resources will be decided by food production. Three questions arise:

1 How much water is needed, in order to ensure the future food supply?
2 Which water will be used in the future to produce this additional food? Will it be irrigation water, i.e. blue water, or natural precipitation, i.e. green water?
3 Can improved use of the water resources defuse the conflict that exists between agriculture and nature in the provision of important services for mankind and Earth's life-support system?

8.1   How much water will we need in the future?

Equipped with the basic evaluations from Chapter 6, estimating our future water needs is not particularly difficult. This is valid at least until the middle of the next century. After that, developments in climate and in population cannot yet be estimated with any certainty.

There are two tasks that must be considered in estimating how much water will be needed to feed the population of 9.5 billion people in 2050. Firstly, we must end hunger by then. This is first and foremost a humanitarian task. But achieving this is a central prerequisite for the future sustainable management of water. In particular, it is unrealistic to expect that people who are hungry could use their environment and water resources sustainably and that they could target their actions towards the prosperity of future generations.

Secondly, the additional people must be provided with food.

Thus, the task is to provide this amount of water together with the respective food to all people who currently use less than 1300 m^3 of green water flow per year, and additionally to unlock these resources for the newly added population. Table 12 lists the results of these considerations and provides information about the green water flow that will be needed in 2050 to provide enough food for all the people on Earth.

As was described in Chapter 6.4, the present green water consumption is already 1200 km^3 per person per year. Three assumptions are made in Table 12 for the further increase:

1   The per-capita use of green water for feeding the population in the prosperous countries will stay at today's high level and not decrease.
2   The people in the developing countries will not increase

Purpose	Green water flow 2050 (km3/year)
Present food supply	7800
Eradication of hunger	2200
Food supply for an additional 3 billion people	3900
Total	13,900

Table 12   Green water flow needed to feed the estimated world
population in 2050

their per-capita use of green water over the base value of
1300 m^3 per year.

3   The amount of green water that is needed to produce the
3000 kcal per day that every person needs does not change.

Given these assumptions, Earth's life-support system must
provide an additional 6100 km^3 on top of the 7800 km^3 per year
that it already has to provide for agriculture in 2050. This brings
us to the second question that needs to be answered.

8.2   Where will the additional water come from?

The immediate answer to this question, in spite of the somewhat
less than positive experience with the Aral Sea, would be to use
more blue water for irrigation and thus, massively expand the
irrigated areas. This assumes firstly that there is enough blue
water available, and secondly that there is enough land available
for irrigation.

Can the irrigated areas be expanded? More than half of
today's irrigated areas are in Asia, mainly in China and India.
They provide 80% of the present grain harvest in China and half

of that in India. The irrigation water, initially taken from the rivers, is now increasingly extracted from the groundwater due to increased global demand. Groundwater levels are dropping rapidly worldwide. This not only increases pumping costs but also leads to the abandonment of many irrigated areas due to water shortages.

The Food and Agriculture Organization of the United Nations (FAO, 2002) dealt in detail with the suggestion of expanding irrigated areas in the next thirty years. According to them, the irrigated areas, especially in developing countries, will expand. At present they occupy 200 million hectares and according to the FAO, they will increase by 2030 to 242 million hectares. These values are net areas, the considerable losses that occur in such areas due to salinization or falling groundwater levels are already accounted for in these numbers. For these reasons, the predicted worldwide increase in irrigated areas will be rather moderate. In fact, the increase in the next thirty years is estimated at only 0.6% per year and thus, will grow only half as fast as the population. A clear signal of the general decline of land reserves can also be seen in the fact that the expansion of irrigated areas is already slowing down, after having more than doubled between 1969 and 2000. The reason for this is that those countries that need the additional irrigated areas the most because of increasing population, i.e. India and China, have already developed the available areas. In the developed countries also, the growth of irrigated areas has slowed down considerably and is now under 0.3% per year.

Even if the supply of irrigation water in the developed countries is not an urgent problem, individual regions in the developing countries will face extreme shortages in the future. In southern Africa for example, where there would be enough land for irrigation, the reduction in precipitation due to climate change will most likely hinder the expansion of irrigated areas. This leads us to the next question as to whether enough water for additional irrigation would be available. This will vary widely between regions. According to this study, in 2030, due to the expansion of irrigation, every fifth developing country will be at or already past its limits of available blue water for irrigation. These regions will then, as Saudi Arabia and Libya already do today, have to extract a large part of their irrigation water from fossil groundwater. They include such populous regions as the West Indies, South Asia, the Near East, and northern Africa. Thus, the results of the FAO study are in close agreement with those of the IMWI, in terms of the possibilities for expanding irrigation.

Overall, the FAO's study, which only goes up to 2030, comes to the conclusion that additional irrigated areas will generally be established where the food is needed, namely in the arid regions of the developing countries. However, these regions also have the greatest water shortages. Additional irrigation will become increasingly difficult since large amounts of water will have to be taken out of fossil groundwater at ever-increasing depths. At the same time, large areas will be lost to agriculture due to salinization. Let us assume that in spite of this, the expansion of irrigated areas increases at the slow rate of 0.6% per year until 2050. Then, 345 million hectares of irrigated land will be available. For the expanded area of irrigation, water will be needed that must also be taken out of the blue water flow. The amount of water needed is estimated to be approximately 600–800 km^3 per year.

Of the total 6100 km^3 per year of green water flow that will be additionally needed in 2050 to feed the population, irrigation can obviously only provide about one-tenth. The clear message from the FAO is this: the expansion of the irrigated areas alone will not solve the problem. A deficit of 5400 km³ per year of green water flow remains, which must be additionally provided to feed the population.

What to do? Let us ignore for the moment the increase in efficiency of water use in agriculture, which will be dealt with in question 3. In principle, there are two options available to obtain this amount of green water:

1   Expansion of rain-fed agriculture, i.e. the form of agriculture which relies on precipitation, and for it to be expanded to areas that have not been used for agriculture up to now.
2   Increased water consumption in the areas that are currently used for rain-fed agriculture, by diverting the water from neighboring ecosystems to the fields. For example, this could be done by clearing a forest and using the water that, as shown in Fig. 18, would then be part of the surface flow, to irrigate new fields nearby.

After the massive land-use changes of the last 300 years (see Chapter 5), there is hardly any room to further expand the areas under rain-fed agriculture. Climate change will not be able to contribute much to this either. Due to increases in temperature, permafrost regions will thaw and the vegetation belt will move north. This is linked to a northward displacement of the Taiga conifer belt also. Purely theoretically, that would create space for new fields, which would connect to the current northern boundary of agriculture. The probable temperature increase in the next decades will ensure the necessary warmth for the crops. However, nothing will change with respect to the second necessary factor that the crops need in spite of the temperature increase. The low solar radiation and short vegetation periods only allow low yields in these areas and thus low agriculturally-used green water flow. In addition, the extent to which climate change in other regions on Earth, e.g. the Mediterranean, will cause accelerated desertification and thus destroy existing agricultural areas is still unknown.

Thus, significant expansion of agriculture in Europe, Russia, North America, and Oceania is most likely no longer possible. Various countries in Africa, such as Angola, as well as Brazil, still have limited areas suitable for agriculture. However, as the current discussion, especially in Brazil, on the generation of renewable energy from raw materials has shown, there is strong competition for using these areas between food production and generation of energy. Brazil is planning to massively expand the production of ethanol from sugar cane in the next twenty-five years. New agricultural areas are to be used for producing ethanol equivalent to half of current Saudi oil production. Brazil would then be, after Saudi Arabia, the second largest energy supplier on Earth. To do this, large amounts of green water flow will have to be diverted so they will no longer be available either for natural ecosystems or for food production.

Changing the land use of neighboring ecosystems to harvest blue water has a severe impact upon the capabilities of these ecological buffer areas. Wherever it could be done, it has already been done in the last 300 years and thus cannot be further expanded on a large scale. The remaining areas will be definitively needed to ensure the integrity of the Earth's life-support system.

The classic courses of action with which the consequences of the population growth were countered in the past 300 years, no longer work. The areas that provided evaporation and could be additionally used to feed an increasing population are no longer available. Already today, our water resources do not fit into such outdated stereotypical thinking.

8.3   Using water better: more crop per drop

Now to the third issue: the only way out appears to be curbing water consumption in agriculture, while simultaneously increasing food production. That means saving water. This is a well-known demand from other areas of sustainability discussion. For instance, in traffic: cars should have better gas mileage rates and thus get more miles per gallon.

In hydrology this is called "more crop per drop." It was coined by the former UN Secretary-General Kofi Annan during the Millennium Conference in 2000. However, the demand for "more crop per drop" is quite different that saving gas. That is just trying to make a non-renewable energy source last longer before it is completely depleted. For the first time, the economical use of water means a global and also sustainable management of a cycle of matter of the Earth system: The water cycle.

Admittedly, this is not an easy task. Keeping the use of green and blue water for food production at today's level, or even better at a lower level, and yet at the same time using that amount of water to produce twice the amount of food will be hard. This goal goes far beyond the green revolution of the 1960s to the 1990s, in which global yields were increased so successfully (see Fig. 22).

The green revolution did not have to worry very much about efficiency in food production. At that time there were neither land nor water shortages. The green revolution could build upon the three following instruments:

1   New, successfully bred high-yield strains of rice, grain, and corn.
2   The expansion of the use of green and blue water flow.
3   Worldwide expansion of areas under cultivation.

The increase in food production attainable using the classical method of simply expanding the use of resources was largely exhausted by this. As we saw above, two of the three options that made the green revolution so successful in producing food for a growing population are now only available on a limited basis: increasing the use of the green and blue water flow and expanding the area under cultivation. Against the background of a population increase to up to eleven billion people, these two options can no longer contribute much to a sustainable and economic management of the global water cycle.

Therefore, we should concentrate on what possibilities exist for using the blue and green water flows more efficiently. Is the potential here even sufficient enough to stabilize water resources and allow sustainable use in the future?

To estimate these possibilities, let's take a closer look at today's yields and compare what is achieved with what is possible. This is presented in Fig. 29 with examples from corn yields from African savanna regions north and south of the equator. These regions are globally problematic. If we conclude that these regions, which presently are characterized by inadequate food supply and variable precipitation, have a chance, then we can be cautiously optimistic for the rest of the world.

Fig. 29 shows four groups of farm types and their respective corn yields. These four types are the small family farms at the bottom end of the possibilities, the average or normal farms in the countries considered, model farms run by well-educated farmers or research farms run by scientists, and commercial, industrialized farms. The majority of the farms are in the first category: family farms with little and often poor land, many children and limited production conditions. For these farmers, in addition to the amount of precipitation, the seed, and the quality of the soil, many more factors play an important part in

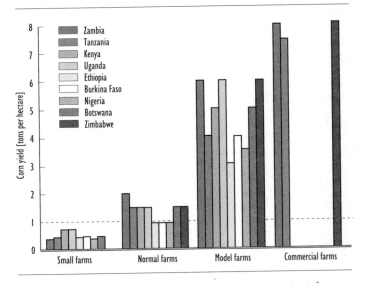

Figure 29 Yield of different farms in African savanna countries (after
Falkenmark, 2004)

the actual yield of their land. These include a lack of workers,
an undefined structure of ownership, limited financial resources,
no access to machinery and water, poor access to the markets
for selling their goods, poor storage facilities for the yield, and
last but not least, their own poor education. The credit that
they received in time to buy the seed, the road that was built to
transport the goods to market, and the local advisor who helps
advance progress all have much more influence upon the manner
in which these farmers till their land and handle water resources
than the seed or precipitation. The social, economic and institutional framework, although it has little to do with nature, influences when the farmers sow their seeds, whether they use the

correct fertilizer, whether they use pesticides correctly and on time, and whether they till the soil correctly in order to maximize the infiltration of the rainwater and thus the green water flow. Nature reacts to deficits with lower yields. As we can see, the small farmers in all the countries have a corn yield of approximately one half-ton per hectare.

The second category in Fig. 29 shows the average corn yield obtained by farmers in southern Africa. In addition to the small farmers, the middle and large farms, usually with better soils, are included here. Here, the average yield is one ton per hectare. Considering the model farms and the research farms in these countries is much more interesting. These farms do not all have better soils and, in principle, work with the same agricultural practices that the smaller and middle farms do. However, the research farms are managed so that they try and obtain the highest yields in the given climatic conditions and the technical possibilities that the smaller and middle-sized farms have. Above all, they try to ensure an optimal temporal sequence of work phases, such as preparing the soil, sowing, fertilizing, weeding, and harvesting, an improved dosage of fertilizers and pesticides, and last but not least, a better choice of seed. The success is astounding. The model farms show that even given the climatic conditions of the African savannas and only using generally-available techniques, yields of three to six tons of corn per hectare can be obtained. Thus, the consistent efficiency-oriented management of the fields using conventional, locally-available technologies produced a greater increase in the yield than the use of higher-yielding seeds and fertilizers during the green revolution. And the best part is: this massive increase in yield did not use a single additional drop of green water. The model farms, like the neighboring smaller farms, only use precipitation for the growth of the crops.

The fourth category in Fig. 29 shows the yield of the so-called commercial farms in Zambia, Tanzania, and Zimbabwe. These large estates usually have the best soils in the region and are operated by well-educated and well-trained experts in accordance with European standards and with advanced technical means. Only the countries listed have a significant number of these large, commercial farms. They achieve corn yields of eight tons per hectare and thus almost the same yield as such large farms in the EU. The grain yield for corn in 2005 was approximately 8.4 tons per hectare (EUROSTAT, 2007). Even these values are far less than the theoretical maximal yield that corn could have. The maximal yield of the crops used today could be, under optimal growth conditions, almost twenty tons per hectare. However, given the different environmental conditions, the many possible pest infestations, and the variable climatic conditions, this will never be achieved on a large scale.

Nevertheless, an important conclusion can be drawn from Fig. 29: the yields that the farmers achieve worldwide now and what they could achieve using the same amount of green water are worlds apart. One world is the 1-ton-per-hectare small farm that will not be able to feed the world's population in the future; the other world is the 5-ton-per-hectare model farm that theoretically would be able to. Both worlds are often only a few kilometers apart and differ mainly in the fact that the managers of the model farms have the capability to deal with the special character of their land very specifically and to consider this in selecting their crops, in choosing farming practices, and in applying fertilizers and pesticides. Access to the land is not what separates both worlds, but rather access to education and secure earnings.

Thus, there is formidable unused potential to increase the yield of fields already under rain-fed cultivation. The reason for the wide deviation between the yields actually achieved and those possible yields is neither the plants nor the climate, but rather the inadequate use of farming techniques by the farmers to maximize the yield.

If one could achieve the increase in yield shown in Fig. 29 worldwide, a doubling of food production could be obtained without requiring more green water flow from the Earth system. How can this happen? Two levers control the more efficient use of precipitation. The first possible way of increasing yields in rain-fed agriculture is in breeding or genetically engineering plants. This aims at producing more biomass or more food with the same productive green water flow. Halbrock (2007) reported in detail on the prospects in breeding and genetic engineering that could decisively increase the productivity of crops. First and foremost, the first step would be to increase the efficiency of photosynthesis, which currently converts only 1% of sunlight into food with the help of the chlorophyll molecule. If this efficiency could be increased to 2%, without requiring more water for the plants, two harvests would be possible in Central Europe, indeed in all temperate zones. However, since the chlorophyll molecule is one of the oldest molecules in evolution, which has hardly changed since the beginning of life on Earth, most scientists assume that an appreciable increase in the efficiency of photosynthesis is as unlikely as the commercial use of nuclear fusion to generate energy. If it were possible, evolution would have probably already increased it by now.

Another approach is to breed for a higher harvest index, which is the fraction of the plant that is grain, in the biomass produced. An increase in the harvest index of the produced biomass has always been one of the urgent breeding goals. Nowadays, the high-yield grain cultivators have a harvest index of over 50%. It is estimated that the upper limit is around 60%, since the plant, in addition to grain, must also produce stalks and leaves and other organs indispensable to its life. Thus, this option for increasing yield without raising water consumption is for the most part exhausted and incapable of providing the doubling of food production required.

Essentially, the third possibility to increase the yield is based on better use of precipitation for plant growth. Plants take up the productive green water flow from the soil and send it to the leaves, where it then undergoes transpiration. However, precipitation is also directed into unproductive green water flow, which is the evaporation of precipitation from the surface of the soil. Increasing yield without changing green water flow can only be achieved by channeling more green water through the plants and decreasing evaporation from the ground. In order to achieve this, the unproductive green water flow must be reduced in favor of the productive flow. Generally, this happens by the farmer providing for dense plant coverage. After or during rain, the precipitation runs down the leaves and the evaporation losses are minimized due to their shading of the soil. Thus, the plant itself provides for more productive water to generate biomass. Although this type of evaporation management is not yet widely distributed worldwide, it has considerable potential. However, careful preparation and maintenance of the plant canopy is required and it is not applicable for all crops. For example, rice, which is mainly grown as wet rice on flooded fields, has very high unproductive water losses, which cannot be reduced. For this reason, an intensive search for a high-yield dry strain of rice is underway.

The productivity of the green water used, i.e. the biomass that can be produced with a certain amount of green water, increases with increasing yield. The more biomass a field produces, the less water is used. The productivity increase obeys the economic law of diminishing marginal utility. This means that with each further increase in yield the increase in the productivity of the water decreases. With a yield increase from 2.5 to 5 tons, the productivity of the green water used in terms of "crop per drop" is thus larger, as compared to an increase from 5 tons to 7.5 tons. At the very latest with a yield of about 10 tons per hectare, the point is reached in which no further productivity increase in using green water is possible. Then, the green water is at optimum use. This important perception means that very intensive agriculture, as practiced in Europe, is the most efficient method of using the green water flow.

How realistic are the prospects of moving from today's one-ton world into the 5-ton-per-hectare world or even the 10-ton-per-hectare world and how can the largest amount of water be provided for nature?

Such yield increases synchronous to productivity increases in using green water cannot be achieved equally advantageously all over the world, as shown by the examples in Fig. 29 from the African savannas. This approach cannot be applied in areas with too little precipitation. The same is true for regions where the yields are already quite high and cannot be increased without additional water. Thus, international experts estimate that worldwide only about 1500 km^3 per year can be saved through increases in productivity in the use of green water flow. That is actually quite a bit of water and corresponds to about a third of the green water flow that is used in rain-fed agriculture today. This means that of the 5400 km^3 of green water flow which must be provided in spite of the expansion in irrigation, in order to feed the world's population in 2050, 1500 km^3 per year could be saved through "more crop per drop." Thus, 3900 km^3 per year of green water flow remains to be provided. Where should the water come from, if no additional areas are available? This deficit in green water, which cannot be significantly reduced any further, expresses the world water crisis that we can expect in the next decades as a plain number.

Symptoms of a water crisis can also be seen in other areas. As we saw before, the water footprint of the residents of the Baltic is twice the size of the area in which they live. This is not a sustainable use of the environment. In their case, this is because they need a large amount of virtual water to heat their homes and at the moment have to obtain it in a non-sustainable way, i.e. by using fossil fuels. This cannot be maintained in the long run. What about the sustainable use of the water resources in other regions on Earth? Corresponding studies on the water footprint of other populations still have to be carried out. Most likely, the conclusions will be similar to the Baltic, even though the reasons will be different due to the respective regional differences.

At present, food production is the largest water user on Earth. Other economic sectors such as the power industry are far behind. This is mostly because there are fossil energy sources that can be exploited, but there is no fossil food that can be mined. By definition, food is a raw material that is 100% renewable. Fossil fuel supplies are rapidly dwindling and their day will be over soon. The conversion to renewable energies has already started. As soon as these energy forms are made of biomass, they are in competition with food production. Then, a further increase in yields over the 5-ton-per-hectare world will be necessary in order to grow crops for energy as well as for food. An easing of the tension is not yet in sight. Thus, the prospects of simply solving the problem by increasing the efficiency of worldwide food production just in developing countries are basically nil.

8.4 Ways to achieve the sustainable use of water resources

Therefore, new ways to increase the water use efficiency are needed in order to provide for the 3900 km^3 of green water flow still lacking in the current account for 2050. Simply continuing to accept hunger and starvation is not an option and neither is abandoning the long-term goal of sustainable development.

There are potentials for increasing the efficiency of use that have not yet been considered. For example, in all previous discussions of the topic, the different uses of precipitation have been dealt with separately. This was particularly striking in respect of irrigation and dry farming. Worldwide, there is tremendous potential to increase the efficiency of water used for irrigation. Presently, irrigation water is generally used very ineffectively, since a large part of the water evaporates unproductively, as seen in the example of wet rice. Underground drip irrigation facilities are much more effective. They transport the irrigation water and the dissolved fertilizer through a branched system of pipes in the root zone directly to the roots. This achieves the same water-use productivity as European high-yield agriculture, since all of the water used is absorbed by the roots and thus, is available to the plants for transpiration. So, with a minimum use of water, high yields are produced.

The increase in productivity is even more impressive if these irrigation systems are utilized in regions in which rain-fed agriculture is indeed possible but where additional water is needed to increase the yield. Here, precipitation provides for the basic water requirements of the plants and irrigation water is used solely to increase the yield.

One could argue that these complex technologies are too expensive and complicated for large parts of the world. This frequently-used argument misjudges the dynamics with which other, more complex technologies, such as computers, the Internet, cars, and many more have conquered the world in no time. Countries such as China and India have the economic power to install these or similar systems on large scales, and they have the education systems in order to teach large segments of the population how to use them.

This example shows that through the integration of irrigation and rain-fed agriculture, water can be used much more efficiently. There are multiple possibilities for achieving increased efficiency of water use through such integration. Several possibilities are already being considered; more are still only figments of the imagination. However, the prerequisite for all of them is that they consistently follow the integrated approach of the guiding principles on water use set down in the Dublin Statement on Water and Sustainable Development.

Trading with virtual water is a part of this. Trading virtual water certainly cannot aim at disrupting agriculture in whole countries by importing all edible goods. One of the basic principles should still be that water should be used where it is needed. However, as we saw in Chapter 7, by trading with virtual water, real water can be saved. This is always the case if the exporter can produce the food more efficiently, water-wise, than the importer. Already today, 25 per cent of the entire trade in grain is due to lack of water. The trade is carried out mainly by countries in desert regions with prosperous populations. Even though many countries will suffer from water scarcity, will they have the resources to buy food from other countries? As least the lack of precipitation in these countries is typically associated with a surplus of sunshine. Generating renewable energy from solar radiation could be an alternative income source for developing countries, just as tourism is for Egypt today. This presumes a consistent internationalization of the food and energy markets.

Thus, trading with virtual water is a part of the management of global water resources. Global management of water resources is a task for the entire population of the planet, just the same as protecting the climate.

Precipitation is the resource that must be managed. It moves as water vapor through the atmosphere, doesn't follow national borders, and even crosses oceans. Against the background of apparent scarcity of water resources, there is no sense in continuing to manage the blue and green water flows, which both originate from precipitation, either regionally or nationally. In the future, as now, there will always be regions on Earth with surplus water, and others with too little. It will prove to be a fortunate coincidence if those with lots of water suffer from a lack of energy, and vice versa. A sustainable world order is bound to balance these deficits against each other, instead of instigating national autarchy at the expense of nature. The industrial nations are doing this now, in that they use fossil fuels and thus increase the CO_2 in the atmosphere; as do the developing countries, in that they destroy their water systems and soils in order to produce food.

Within the next forty-five years, the challenge to find an additional green water flow of 3900 km³ per year without damaging the Earth's life-support system will still be there. Many roads lead there, and all of them are complex. A few are already visible on the horizon:

1 Intelligent saving by using integration gains. This assumes that experts from various disciplines seek solutions together – not a strong suit in most of the classic sciences. Initial large-scale projects have been set up under the German Federal Ministry for Education and Research under the name "Global Change and the Hydrological Cycle"

(GLOWA, 2007). The research is targeted at identifying possibilities for integration gains in different regions in Europe and Africa through combined land and water management to research ways for future sustainable handling of water and to develop courses of action to conduct them.

2 Area expansion. This is only possible as a limited measure, without damaging the Earth system. Will people do it anyway? Unfortunately, there is quite a bit of evidence that shows that they will, and in addition to the classic expansion areas on land, there is now also more ocean area being used in the course of expanding aquaculture.

3 Increased usage of water-surplus areas and trade with virtual water. Why shouldn't agriculture in Europe, the USA, Canada – in the future, also in Russia and the Ukraine – produce surplus food in increasing measure? We saw that this is for the most part possible in fertile soils while maintaining sustainable standards. No other large-scale agriculture works more efficiently with water than that in Europe. From this point of view, it is better for the Earth system if fields are used intensively where it is possible to do so, instead of using wide areas extensively, where it is actually not possible to do so without destroying them.

The prerequisite for solving the problem is learning to transcend national and cultural borders and to realize the Earth as a whole entity, not just abstractly and philosophically, but in reality. Our first steps have been taken. Here, they lead us back to the example of the Nile catchment area.

In Chapter 3 we encountered the large asymmetry between the Nile countries. Whereas Egypt is totally dependent upon the Nile water and actually does not have any significant renewable water resources, Ethiopia is a rich in water resources. As an upstream riparian country, Ethiopia also has control over Egyptian water resources. This has led to decades of conflicts and unrest between both countries, which among others have been instigated by Egypt in order to impede Ethiopia's development and keep it weak.

In order to end these conflicts, in 1999 the Nile Basin Initiative (NBI), for regional cooperation of all countries in the Nile basin, was created. The goal is a joint long-term development and management of the water resources of the river. Through increased cooperation, real advantages for all are to be achieved within the catchment area and a basis for mutual trust will be created.

Thus, the economical and geographical asymmetry will be balanced through cooperation and not through conflict. Egypt is economically much stronger than the upstream countries, such as Ethiopia. They, however, are stronger geographically: they have the water. Both sides, upstream and downstream, have recognized that there are enough water resources available to develop agriculture in Ethiopia and in the other upstream countries, and still leave Egypt with enough water. Both sides win through intelligent, coordinated, common use of the Nile. Trust has developed and it has been agreed that not only should the water use be coordinated, but also the electricity networks and the exchange of energy. Essential to this approach, which has strong international support, are that they consistently try to find and implement "win-win" situations.

This means that things are happening for the Nile area. National borders are being crossed, water resources are being commonly used in agreement with all, and the same will happen with the other resources. Similar developments are starting in other large catchment areas such as the Volta and the Mekong rivers.

Yet this is just the beginning. There is still much to do before we achieve global management of our water resources. This global management will bring experts who have had little to say to each other, such as hydraulic engineers, hydrologists, farmers, and ecologists, closer together. Along the way, our land resources, what we do with them and what they provide for us will be more and more in the spotlight. Research targeted at identifying which mode of global interaction of the different forms of land resource use is best suited to preserve the services provided by nature, and at the same time to ensure our survival, has just started. The questions that deal with this are among the most fascinating and complex issues in research at the present.

If we learn to manage water resources globally, they will last a long time. Water is not like crude oil: it renews itself constantly. Water, the natural resource that is most likely to become scarce first, will be the resource to show us if we are capable of sustainably managing the Earth system's important cycles of matter. Only in this way can we do justice to the responsibility that we have already acquired through appropriation and possession. More and more scientists and technicians from around the world are addressing these topics, more and more politicians are asking for solutions, and more and more people need a solution.

Glossary

Biomass: The amount of living matter created by a plant through the assimilation of CO_2 with the help of sunlight. There is wet and dry, and above-ground and underground, biomass. In the context of plant production in connection with green water flow, dry above-ground biomass is usually meant.

Desertification: Process of expansion of deserts due to over-utilization of desert margins by humans.

Dielectric constant (synonymous term: relative permittivity) is a measure of the asymmetric distribution of positive and negative electric charges in a molecule. It assumes a value of 1 if both charges are equally distributed. The dielectric constant increases with the degree of separation of the positive and negative charges in the different parts of the molecule.

Downstream: means the regions of a river system located in a hydraulically-lower location than a given position along a stream or river. A section of the river system is hydraulically lower if gravity transports the water in the direction of or nearer to the mouth of the stream or river.

Earth life-support system: Part of the Earth system that provides the requirements for life as we know it. Life is only possible in a specific and limited temperature interval and is linked to the presence of CO_2 and liquid water.

Earth system: Sum of all minerals and interaction of cycles of matter on Earth. The most important cycles of matter are the water cycle, the carbon cycle, and the nitrogen, phosphorus and sulfur cycle. The Earth system receives its energy from the Sun and to a small degree from internal processes in the interior of the planet. Energy uptake and energy loss are in equilibrium. The equilibrium temperature is largely determined by the greenhouse gases of the atmosphere.

Eolian deflation: Erosion of the Earth's surface by the removal of fine-grain particles by the wind.

Eutrophication: An uncontrolled increase in chemical nutrients in an ecosystem.

FAO: Food and Agricultural Organization of the United Nations based in Rome (www.fao.org).

Global Water Partnership: established by the World Bank, the UNDP, and the Swedish Development Agency in 1996 in order to foster the implementation of the Dublin Principles of an integrated and sustainable use of water (www.gwpforum.org).

Greenhouse gases (GHG): Constituents of the atmosphere that reduce the loss of heat into space, which, depending on their concentration, would lead to a cooling of the Earth. The most effective greenhouse gases in the atmosphere are water vapor and CO_2. They increase the temperature of the Earth's surface by about 30°C.

Harvest index: The ratio of yield biomass to the total cumulative biomass at harvest in percent. The remainder consists of leaves, stems and ears.

IWMI: International Water Management Institute located in Colombo, Sri Lanka. IWMI's task is to conduct basic research in the area of water management *(www.iwmi.org)*.

Land use: The purposeful interference of humans in natural processes at the Earth's surface in order to gain direct benefit from it. Besides changes in vegetation, e.g. from forests to agriculture, settlements, streets, etc. this also includes intensifying the growth of pastures and meadows with artificial fertilizers.

Natural resources: To survive, mankind is dependent upon the constant availability of goods and services provided by the Earth system, which are called natural resources.

Soil moisture: Water content in the soil, generally given as volume percent (Vol.-%). The soil can hold water against gravity due to bonding forces of the contained minerals. A fraction of this water can be used by plants. This is a prerequisite for plant growth.

UNEP: United Nations Environment Programme based in Nairobi (www.unep.org).

UNESCO: United Nations Educational, Scientific and Cultural Organization located in Paris (*www.unesco.org*).

Upstream: The regions of a river system located in the direction opposite to the flow of a stream from a given position. A section of the river system is hydraulically higher, if gravity transports the water away from the given location.

WHO: World Health Organization of the United Nations, based in Geneva (*www.who.int*).

References

Allan, J. A. (1993): "Fortunately there are substitutes for water otherwise our hydro-political futures would be impossible," In: ODA, *Priorities for water resources allocation and management*, ODA, London, pp. 13–26.

Alcamo, J., Vörösmarty, C. (2005): "A new Assessment of World Water Resources and their Ecosystem Services," *Global Water News*, No. 1 (2005) 2 (www.gwsp.org vom 12. 8. 2005).

Brown, L. R. (2004): *Outgrowing the Earth*, W. W. Norton & Co., London.

Cosgrove, W. J., Rijsberman, F. R. (2000): *World Water Vision – Making Water Everybody's Business*, Earthscan, London.

Daily, G. C. (Ed) (1997): *Nature's Services – Human Dependence on Natural Ecosystems*, Island Press, Washington D.C.

ECOSOC (2001): Statistical Profiles of LDCs, 2001. Economic and Social Council (ECOSOC), United Nations Conference on Trade and Development UNCTAD, http://www.unctad.org/en/pub/ldcprofiles2001.en.htm (1. 10. 2002).

EUROSTAT (2007): Viewed 6. 12. 2006 at http://epp.eurostat.ec.europa.eu

Ellen, R. F. (1987): *Environment, Subsistance and System. The Ecology of Small-scale Social Formations*, Cambridge, 324 pp.

Falkenmark, M. (2001): More Crops or More Ecological Flow?
– in Search of a "Golden Section" in Catchment Rainwater
Partitioning, in: Proceedings of the SIWI Seminar "Water
Security for Cities, Food and Environment – Towards
Catchment Hydrosolidarity" Stockholm, 2001.

Falkenmark, M., Rockström, J. (2004): *Balancing Water for
Humans and Nature*, Earthscan, London.

Fewtrell L., Kaufmann R. B., Kay D., Enanoria W., Haller
L., Colford J. M. Jr. (2005): "Water, sanitation, and
hygiene interventions to reduce diarrhoea in less developed
countries: a systematic review and meta-analysis." *Lancet
Infectious Diseases* 5(1): 42–52.

FAO (1995): *Irrigation in Africa in Figures*, Water Reports No.
7, Rome, FAO.

FAO (1999): IFAD/FAO (1999). Prevention of land degradation,
enhancement of carbon sequestration and conservation
of biodiversity through land use change and sustainable
land management with a focus on Latin America and the
Caribbean. World Soil Resources Reports 86. Rome, Food
and Agriculture Organization.

FAO (2002): World Agriculture: towards 2015/30, Summary
Report, Viewed 5. 1. 2007 at http://www.fao.org/004/y3557e/
y3557e21.htm

FAO (2006): World Agriculture: towards 2050, Summary
Report, Viewed 3. 1. 2007 at http://www.fao.org/es/esd/
at2050web.pdf

Geographie (2007): Gebhardt, H., Glaser, R., Radtke,
U., Reuber, P. (Hrsg.) (2007): *Geographie – Physische
Geographie und Humangeographie*, Spektrum
Akademischer Verlag, Heidelberg.

Gleick, P. H. (2000): *The World's Water 2000–2001. The Biennial Report on Fresh water Resources*, Island Press, Washington D.C.

Gleick, P. H. (2005): Viewed 6. 12. 2006 at http://www.aaas.org/international/ehn/fisheries/gleick.htm

GLOWA (2007): Projekt: Globaler Wandel des Wasserkreislaufs im Rahmen der Global Change Forschung des Bundesministeriums für Bildung und Forschung (BMBF), viewed 10. 1. 2007 at http://www.glowa.org

Global Water Partnership (2000): Integrated Water Resources Management, Technical Advisory Committee (TAC) Background Paper No. 4 (www.gwpforum.org on 3. 9. 2005).

Gorshkov, V. G., Gorshkov V. V., Makarieva, A. M. (2000): *Biotic Regulation of the Environment: Key Issue of Global Change*. Springer-Verlag, London.

Halbrock, K. (2007): *Feeding the Planet: Environmental Protection through Sustainable Agriculture*, Fischer Taschenbuch Verlag, Frankfurt am Main.

Hoekstra, A. Y. and Hung, P. Q. (2002): Virtual water trade: A quantification of virtual water flows between nations in relation to international crop trade, Value of Water Research Report Series No. 11, IHE, Delft, the Netherlands.

IWMI (2000): International Water Management Institute: Water Issues of 2025: A Research Perspective. Colombo, Sri Lanka.

IPCC (Intergovernmental Panel on Climate Change) (2001): Scientific Assessment of Climate Change, Summary for Policymakers, Climate Change 2001: Synthesis Report of the IPCC Third Assessment Report. XVIII Session of the IPCC, Wembley, United Kingdom, 24–29 September 2001.

Jäger, J. (2007): *Our Planet: How Much More Can Earth Take?*, Fischer Taschenbuch Verlag, Frankfurt am Main.

Jansson, Å., Folke, C., Rockström, J., and Gordon, L.
    (1999): "Linking fresh water flows and ecosystem services
    appropriated by people: The case of the Baltic Sea drainage
    basin." *Ecosystems*, 2, 351–366.

Latif, M. (2007): *Climate Change: The Point of No Return*,
    Fischer Taschenbuch Verlag, Frankfurt am Main.

Mason S. A. (2004): *From Conflict to Cooperation in the
    Nile Basin*, Dissertation, Center for Security Studies, ETH
    Zürich.

Nicol A. (2003): *The Nile: Moving beyond Cooperation*,
    IHP-VI, Technical Documents in Hydrology, PC-CP Series,
    No. 16, UNESCO, Geneva.

Oki, T., Sato, M., Kawamura, A., Miyake, M., Kanae, S.,
    Musiake, K. (2003): "Virtual water trade to Japan and in
    the world." In: *Virtual water trade. Proceedings of the
    International Expert Meeting on Virtual Water Trade* (Ed.:
    A. Y. Hoekstra), Value of Water Research Report Series No.
    12, Delft University, Holland.

Rapp A., Murray-Rust, H., Christiansson, C., Berry, L. (1972):
    "Soil Erosion and Sedimentation in four Catchments near
    Dodima, Tanzania", *Geografiska Annaler*, 54A (1972), 3–4,
    pp. 255–318.

SDNP (2006): Sustainable Development Network Programme
    viewed 3. 12. 2006 at http://www.sdnpbd.org/sdi/
    international_days/wed/2006/desertification/unep_status.
    htm#global_stat_dsrt

Shiklomanov, I. A., (Ed.) (1997): *Assessment of water resources
    and water availability in the world. Comprehensive
    Assessment of the fresh water resources of the world*, World
    Meteorological Organization, Geneva.

Shiklomanov, I. A. (2000): "Appraisal and assessment of world
    water resources", *Water International*, 25(1): 11–32.

SIWI (Stockholm International Water Institute) (2004): *Securing Sanitation – The Compelling Case to Address the Crisis*, Report to Government of Norway, The Stockholm International Water Institute, Sweden.

SIWI (Stockholm International Water Institute) (2005): *UN Millennium Project Task Force on Water and Sanitation, Final Report, Abridged Edition Health, Dignity, and Development: What Will It Take?*, Stockholm International Water Institute, Sweden.

Steffen, W., Sanderson, A., Jäger, J., Tyson, P. D., Moore III, B., Matson, P. A., Richardson, K., Oldfield, F., Schellnhuber, H.-J., Turner II, B. L., Wasson, R. J. (2004): *Global Change and the Earth System – A Planet Under Pressure*, Springer Verlag, Heidelberg, Germany.

UNEP (2002): *Vital Water Graphics – An Overview of the State of the World's Fresh and Marine Waters*, UNEP, Nairobi, Kenya.

UNEP (2005): Severskiy, I., Chervanyov, I., Ponomarenko, Y., Novikova, N. M., Miagkov, S. V., Rautalahti, E. and D. Daler. *Aral Sea, GIWA Regional assessment 24.* University of Kalmar, Sweden.

UNEP/GRID (2006): Viewed 6. 12. 2006 at http://maps.grida.no/

U. S. Census Bureau (2006): World population on 6 December 2006: 6,561,495,011 viewed 6. 12. 2006 at http://www.census.gov/ipc/www/popclockworld.html

Vashneva, N. S. and Peredkov, A. V. (2001). *Water and Health. Water and Sustainable Development of Central Asia*, Soros-Kyrgyzstan Fund (in Russian).

Vitousek, P. M. 1994: "Beyond Global Warming: Ecology and Global Change". *Ecology*: Vol. 75, No. 7, pp. 1861–1876.

Wackernagel, M., Rees, W. (1996): *Our ecological footprint: Reducing human impact on the Earth*, New Society Publishers, Gabriola Island, B.C., Canada.

WBGU (1997): *Welt im Wandel: Wege zu einem nachhaltigen Umgang mit Süßwasser, Jahresgutachten 1997 des Wissenschaftlichen Beirats der Bundesregierung Globale Umweltveränderungen*, Springer Verlag, Heidelberg.

WHO/UNICEF (2004): Joint UNICEF/WHO Monitoring Program (JMP) website at http://www.wssinfo.org/en/welcome.html

Wichelns, D. (2001): "The role of 'virtual water' in efforts to achieve food security and other national goals, with an example from Egypt", *Agricultural Water Management*, 49: 131–151.

Williams, E. D., Ayres, R. U. and Heller, M. (2002): "The 1,7 kilogram microchip: Energy and material use in the production of semiconductor devices", *Environmental Science and Technology* 36 (24): 5504–5510.

WMO (1992): Viewed 25. 10. 2005 at http://www.wmo.ch/web/homs/documents/english/icwedece.html